Legacy of the Puppy

Legacy of the Puppy

THE ULTIMATE ILLUSTRATED GUIDE

Photographs by Hiroyuki Ueki and Toyofumi Fukuda

Text by Hiromi Nakano

Supervising Editor: Tadaaki Imaizumi

Beagle
42 days

CHRONICLE BOOKS

SAN FRANCISCO

First published in the United States in 2004 by Chronicle Books LLC.

Text copyright © 2003 by Hiromi Nakano.
Photographs copyright © 2003 by Hiroyuki Ueki and Toyofumi Fukuda.
English translation copyright © 2004 by Chronicle Books LLC.

Library of Congress Cataloging-in-Publication Data available.

ISBN 0-8118-4534-6

English translation by Isao Tezuka and Izumi Tezuka.
English text design by Janis Reed.

Manufactured in China.

Distributed in Canada by Raincoast Books
9050 Shaughnessy Street
Vancouver, British Columbia V6P 6E5

10 9 8 7 6 5 4 3 2 1

Chronicle Books LLC
85 Second Street
San Francisco, California 94105

www.chroniclebooks.com

Australian shepard
38 days

Contents

Breeds by Group

Individual dogs have distinct personalities, but each breed shares common physical and character traits that have been bred into it. Several were designed to assist livestock farmers, for example (and some among them still do), and others were, and are, suited for hunting. Various kennel clubs throughout the world categorize dog breeds differently; in this book, we have divided them into seven groups.

Herding Group · 12–37

Dogs in this group—herding dogs, cattle dogs, and sheep dogs—were bred for agility, robustness, and intelligence to aid them in protecting cattle from wild animals. Many breeds in this group are sociable and intelligent enough to work alongside humans, and they respond well to structure and order and are at their best when kept busy. Simply speaking, they are workaholics.

Breeds (in alphabetical order)

Australian Kelpie	12
Australian Shepherd	14
Bearded Collie	16
Belgian Sheepdog	18
Border Collie	22
Bouvier des Flandres	24
Cardigan Welsh Corgi	26
Collie	28
German Shepherd	30
Old English Sheepdog	32
Pembroke Welsh Corgi	34
Shetland Sheepdog	36

Collie

Bearded collie

Sporting Group · 38–63

The breeds of this group are often used to hunt birds such as snipes and ducks; each breed has its own specialty. Some are fit for hills and dales, while others are at home in the wetlands and alongside bodies of water. Some are good at tracking and chasing prey, and others excel at retrieving; their sharp senses enable them to react quickly to the presence of game. However, the custom of using a team of several dogs for hunting has also helped these breeds develop temperate dispositions that make them compatible with other dogs and sensitive to human feelings.

Breeds (in alphabetical order)

American Cocker Spaniel	38
Brittany Spaniel	40
Clumber Spaniel	42
English Cocker Spaniel	44
English Pointer	46
English Setter	48
English Springer Spaniel	50
Flat-Coated Retriever	52
Golden Retriever	54
Irish Setter	56
Labrador Retriever	58
Nova Scotia Duck Tolling Retriever	60
Weimaraner	62

English springer spaniel

Irish setter

Hound Group

Dogs in the Hound Group, as opposed to those of the bird-hunting Sporting Group, track larger animals; they are further subdivided into sight hounds and scent hounds. As indicated by their subgroup names, sight hounds are able to spot animals from long distances, and scent hounds have a keen sense of smell, which makes them adept at sniffing animals out. Specialists at tracking animals, the breeds of this group are quick, persistent hunters.

Breeds (in alphabetical order)

Afghan Hound	64
Basenji	66
Basset Hound	68
Beagle	70
Borzoi	72
Dachshund (Miniature)	74
Irish Wolfhound	78
Petit Basset Griffon Vendéen	80
Saluki	82
Whippet	84

Petit basset griffon Vendéen

Saluki

Terrier Group

The breeds of this group, which possess a peculiar trait known as "terrier fire," are hunting dogs bred to ferret out small animals such as foxes, rabbits, and badgers from their lairs. (Their name comes from the Latin term for "earth," or "ground.") To maintain their characteristic appearance, a special grooming technique known as stripping—pulling out dead hair—is necessary. They are agile and alert, and, in spite of their small size, these breeds tend to be aggressive and daring. They also display a unique ability to think independently while tracking and hunting, and they are bright enough to outsmart small animals that threaten crops and livestock. The more you get to know these dogs, the more their fiery dispositions and intelligence will enchant you.

Breeds (in alphabetical order)

Airedale Terrier	86
Bedlington Terrier	88
Border Terrier	90
Bull Terrier	92
Cairn Terrier	94
Jack Russell Terrier	96
Kerry Blue Terrier	98
Lakeland Terrier	100
Miniature Schnauzer	102
Norfolk Terrier	104
Scottish Terrier	106
Sealyham Terrier	108
Soft-Coated Wheaten Terrier	110
Welsh Terrier	112
West Highland White Terrier	114
Wire Fox Terrier	116

West Highland white terrier

Lakeland terrier

Toy Group *118–147*

These small, adorable breeds, culled from the Hound Group, the Sporting Group, and the Terrier Group to form a new category, generally maintain the temperament and appearance characteristic of the group to which they originally belonged. The breeds of this group, though gentle and faithful, are relatively strong for their size but need human protection. Their company is comforting and delightful, and few require much exercise.

Breeds (in alphabetical order)

Brussels Griffon	118
Cavalier King Charles Spaniel	120
Chihuahua	122
Chinese Crested	124
Italian Greyhound	126
Japanese Chin	128
Maltese	130
Manchester Terrier (Toy)	132
Miniature Pinscher	134
Papillon	136
Pekingese	138
Pomeranian	140
Pug	142
Shih Tzu	144
Yorkshire Terrier	146

Shih tzu

Chihuahua

Working Group *148–181*

Many of the breeds in this group, large, powerful animals often used as working dogs, guard dogs, police dogs, or rescue dogs, were grouped together from other categories such as the Herding Group and the Sporting Group. Although they are fundamentally faithful to their owners, subjecting them to rigorous training from the time they are puppies is vital.

Breeds (in alphabetical order)

Akita	148
Alaskan Malamute	150
Bernese Mountain Dog	152
Boxer	154
Bullmastiff	156
Doberman Pinscher	158
Dogo Argentino	160
Giant Schnauzer	162
Great Dane	164
Great Pyrenees	166
Leonberger	168
Newfoundland	170
Rottweiler	172
Saint Bernard	174
Samoyed	176
Siberian Husky	178
Standard Schnauzer	180

Saint Bernard

Leonberger

These breeds, also called utility dogs, come in a variety of sizes and appearances; indeed, the group consists of breeds that do not fit neatly into the other existing categories. Nevertheless, each breed has characteristics appropriate to another group: the poodle, the Lhasa apso, and the French bulldog, for example, could be classified under the Toy Group. Some breeds, too, have features that are found in more than one group.

Breeds (in alphabetical order)

Chow chow

Bulldog

The Ancestors and History of Dogs

By Tadaaki Imaizumi, zoologist

The dog is said to be not only humankind's best friend but also its oldest, and it is very interesting to study what the dog's ancestors looked like and how the species has evolved since it was domesticated. Many puppies seem to look alike and are dark no matter which breed they belong to. This coloring is a common characteristic among the canids, the members of the animal family that includes dogs, and it is nearly impossible to distinguish one young canid from one of another species in that family.

In the wild, young canids have a better chance of survival if they are dark, which makes it difficult for predators to spot them in the dark burrows where they are born and raised. However, since dogs have become domesticated, other colors and color combinations, such as white and parti-color, have also evolved in the young of the species.

One of several theories about the ancestry of dogs is that wolves and early dogs freely interbred and produced fertile hybrid puppies. Under natural conditions today, though, such interbreeding virtually never happens.

Swedish and Chinese scientists who conducted DNA analysis of many dog breeds and of wolves, however, have reported that the domesticated species can be traced back to the wolves of eastern Asia. "Most dogs shared common gene regions that were inherited generation after generation," they concluded. "We discovered that early dogs had in their blood at least four lineages of wolves. Furthermore, we traced back the genotypic branching of dogs in many locations and found that these wolves were most probably domesticated about 15,000 years ago in eastern Asia and then brought to Europe." However, what the researchers mean by "four lineages of wolves" is not clear, because only one species of wolf exists. Because of this ambiguous wording, it is difficult to determine whether this theory is valid.

Another thesis, based on detailed ethological research, suggests that dogs are different than wolves. Dr. Erik Zimen of Germany, who raised a poodle and a wolf, reported that "a grown poodle's behaviors are very much like a young wolf's in many aspects. Both are easy to train when they are young. But once a wolf is grown, it is not easy to train anymore. Unlike dogs, wolves become aggressive as they grow, in order to establish dominance in the pack. They consider the wolf keeper a member of the pack and may attack him when he is off guard, causing serious, unexpected injury. After reaching the age of 2, wolves tend to eliminate strangers from the pack." Zimen concludes that wolves are entirely different animals than dogs.

Anyone who has ever owned a dog has probably noticed that it behaves differently than other canids such as wolves or foxes. Dogs, for one thing, are gentle and obedient. Even if you were to put your fingers in one's mouth or hurt it a little, it would usually not bite. If you were to handle a fox or a raccoon that way, however, you would probably be bitten and possibly severely injured.

Dr. Michael Fox of England reports, "I'm just getting started, but I am working on a comparative study of the behaviors of dogs, wolves, and hybrids between wolves and malamutes. I have found that certain dog behavioral patterns, which are considered dog characteristics, are not observed at all among wild canids like wolves and coyotes. Today's dogs must be related to wolves, but they probably came from an ancestry that is very different from that of wolves. It seems that this ancestry is a wild dog that branched off from a wolf long before humans domesticated dogs."

Morphologically, dogs are totally different than wolves. Although Fox mentions no specific species as dog ancestors, it seems they are descendants of dogs similar to the dingoes, found wild in Australia, and pariah dogs, which live wandering lives in India and other areas of southern Asia. These dogs are believed to be the offspring of wild dogs that branched off from wolves hundreds of thousands of years ago.

A distribution analysis of canids that live in packs shows that gray wolves live in many areas of Asia, but in Southeast Asia, where wolves are not found, there are wild dogs called dholes. This distribution seems to be based on the similar lifestyles of these two canid species, and, according to this train of thought, other wild dogs likely lived in southern and southwestern Asia, where wolves and dholes were rarely found.

Fossil study shows that dogs were domesticated in Southeast Asia more than 20,000 years ago, and specialists have determined that these dogs were clearly different than wolves. In addition, about 10 years ago, a Japanese archaeological expedition unearthed dog fossils at the 35,000-year-old Palmyra ruins in Syria. Finally, carbon dating of wild-dog fossils found at aboriginal campsite ruins in Australia, which revealed the dogs to be similar to modern dingoes, determined the fossils to be about the same age as the Syrian ones.

Finnish vertebrate paleontologist Bjorn Kurten says dogs were domesticated about 35 centuries ago, which is consistent with the Palmyra findings. According to him, in the late Paleolithic period, early Cro-Magnon humans entered Europe after wandering though Africa, southern Asia, and Australia, accompanied by dogs. About 5,000 years later, Neanderthal humans that lived in Europe and most of Asia suddenly disappeared, most likely wiped out by the newcomers.

It seems humans made friends with dogs and prospered because of the abilities of their canine companions. In fact, our species' survival was greatly aided by dogs, which then, as now, were able to find and roust small prey hiding in the bushes and capture larger animals that were able to outrun humans. Living with dogs has become very commonplace for many people today, and although many of us adore them, it would not be a bad idea to appreciate them more.

Photographing Dogs

By Hiroyuki Ueki and Toyofumi Fukuda

A baby swan grows from an awkward, dark-colored cygnet into a graceful, snow-white adult bird. A comparable transformation happens in the world of dogs, too: A puppy with dark coloring may grow up to be a white or golden-brown dog. Given the difference in appearance between puppies and their parents, it is often hard to believe they are related. While photographing dogs for this book, in fact, we were surprised by this curious lack of resemblance.

Puppies are the main characters in this book, which covers a brief and precious time in the course of dogs' lives: Although dogs live, on average, about 15 or 16 years, their days as puppies last only about 3 months. One is seldom privileged to see a mother dog nurse her puppies, and it's even less common with rare breeds. Normally, a nursing mother dog is quite nervous, but, with the help of the owners of the dogs we photographed, we were able to witness these intimate moments. A nursing mother dog has a very tender, gentle look, and puppies, too, are relaxed under their mother's protection. We have captured their quiet moments of tranquility as well as their carefree moments of fun, and we are delighted to share them with our readers.

This project took us 8 long years. If we had been photographing only adult dogs, we could have finished it more quickly, but a puppy book is different. There were times when we had to wait until puppies were born. In other cases, timing was not on our side, and we missed the stage when they are at their cutest.

Time has flown by—some of the puppies we photographed are now 8 or 9 years old—and, every time we see them again after a few years, we are amazed at their growth. It delights us, too, when they wag their tails as if to communicate that they remember us.

The simple but informative text of this book, which describes both adult dogs and puppies, and the large photographs are so appealing that we believe you will pick it up many times. And why do we think you will value it so much? Today, the world is increasingly becoming a digital place that appears to operate only in binary characters of 0 and 1. Technological development cannot be stopped, and the world sometimes seems to be rushing forward at breakneck speed. Although technology has made the world more convenient, appreciation for craftsmanship seems to have decreased; amateurs can now use computers to produce, with relative ease, the same type of work an artist with extensive experience took long hours to create. As a result, some craft-related professions are disappearing.

Where are we heading in such a hurry? We should slow down and take more time to appreciate the world around us. We use the Internet and engage in rhetoric about a paperless society, yet we still continue to produce hard copies of information we obtain on our computers. Why? In contemplating this reality, we realize the importance of books. A book has the ability to spark readers' interest in topics other than the one they set out to read about. It invites them to investigate a broader field of interest. We expect this kind of stimulating role from this book, and we hope it becomes one that readers will like to keep close at hand.

We conclude by thanking the owners of the dogs introduced in this book. Without their cooperation, this project would have been impossible. We also extend our heartfelt appreciation to the editors, designers, and other staff members of the original publishers, Yama-Kei Publishers Co., for their efforts. Thank you.

About This Book

This photographic guide to dogs, classified by group, presents puppies of each breed in various poses and attitudes, with a comparative photograph of a mother dog on each spread. Although it is not easy to take pictures of adult dogs with their young, this book has succeeded in capturing many intimate moments. The ages of the puppies are indicated near each picture.

Breed Data

Information about each breed in this book covers group name, breed name, place or places of origin, height, weight, and coat characteristics and colors. It also includes alternate names, as well as remarks about special considerations for dogs to be presented at dog shows.

Group name: Listed on the left of the first breed name in that group; color coded.

Breed name: The name accepted by the American Kennel Club, or AKC (names used by other kennel clubs, and alternate names, are listed below).

Place(s) of origin: Where the breed was kept or controlled at the time of its recognition as a valid breed.

Height: The measurement from the ground to the base of the neck in the standing position, approximate and based on the average for the breed.

Weight: The measurement of the dog's mass, approximate and based on the average for the breed.

Coat: Characteristics and color of the fur; where space is limited, some colors are omitted.

Also called: Breed names used by the American Kennel Club (AKC), the Kennel Club (KC; United Kingdom), and sometimes the Fédération Cynologique Internationale (FCI; the International Federation of Cynology—the study of the natural history of dogs—based in Belgium but international) are listed. Names used in the place or places of origin, as well as popular names, are also listed when known.

Key

- Large dog (more than 32 inches tall)
- Medium dog (12–24 inches tall)
- Small dog (less than 12 inches tall)
- Barker, or a quiet and cautious dog that barks only at prowlers
- Dog that requires a lot of exercise
- Dog that requires extensive coat care

General Terms

Pure breed: A human-controlled variety officially recognized by a kennel club.

Bitzer: A variety not recognized as a pure breed; bitzers do not have pedigrees.

Household pet: A dog that belongs to a household, including crossbreeds and pure breeds without pedigrees.

Pedigree: A pure-breed certificate that shows three to five generations of ancestry.

Kennel club: An organization whose purpose is to maintain pure breeds and support good relations between dogs and humans. There are two types: one for all breeds and another for specific breeds. The major all-breed kennel clubs, which issue pedigrees, are the AKC, the KC, and the FCI.

Breed: A variety. Various kennel clubs may have different names for a particular breed. Also, in some cases, a breed may be officially recognized by one kennel club but not by another.

Standard: The specifications by which each breed is judged at dog shows. Standards describe the ideal characteristics for each breed, but they are not an absolute condition for a dog's recognition as one of a specific breed.

Australian Kelpie

Place of origin: Australia

Size: [male] Height: 18–20 inches;
weight: 24–31 pounds
[female] Height: 17–29 inches;
weight: 20–24 pounds

Coat: Short, smooth, and dense. Colors
include black, tan, red, chocolate, and
bluish gray.

Also called: Kelpie, Australian sheepdog

AKC/Miscellaneous; KC/Unrecognized

29 days

"Compared with other breeds, Australian kelpies seem to grow faster: their eyes open earlier, their ears stand earlier, and they wean earlier," one owner says.

85 days

The breed's origin and lineage are uncertain, though some people believe its name is derived from the legendary Scottish water sprite; alternatively, it hearkens back to a dog by that name.

Active, intelligent, and hardworking, these natives of their namesake country have great stamina. "They are bustling about all day, and seem to sleep very little," says one owner. "They are very serious, and they will never fail to respond to your call." Appropriately for dogs bred to herd sheep, Australian kelpies are quick to size up situations, and they know when to be aggressive and when to withdraw. As another owner comments, "They don't fail to accomplish what they were asked to do."

On the job, these tough, high-spirited, and zealous sheepdogs can easily run 30 miles a day, so they must be walked long distances or allowed to run freely to satisfy their need for exercise, and it is important to provide them with tasks that engage them both physically and mentally. This highly social breed is easy to train and to teach various games—and fun to play with.

The Australian kelpie's all-weather coat requires little maintenance.

29 days

Australian Shepherd

Place of origin: United States

38 days

38 days

38 days

How these round-faced, flat-eared puppies bounce and prance on their robust little legs! Australian shepherds love to move, but, as one owner points out, when they are puppies, they seem to hop rather than run. "Somehow," he says, "their running motion is up and down." At 1–2 months, their ears stand up, with the ends lopping forward, forming the so-called Aussie ears, and their eyes, dark violet at first, gradually lighten to blue or amber.

Despite its name, the Australian shepherd, which resembles the Border collie, was first bred in the United States. However, its lineage is not clear. It may be the offspring of a dog

38 days

38 days

38 days

Size: [male] Height: 20–23 inches; weight: 50–65 pounds
[female] Height: 18–21 inches weight: 35–50 pounds

Coat: Straight or wavy; undercoat seasonally changes density. Feathering on neck, chest, and forelegs prominent in males. Colors include red merle, blue merle, red, and black, all of which may include white markings or tan points.

Remarks: May have natural bobtail; if not, kennel clubs require docked tail.

AKC/Herding; KC/Pastoral

European immigrants crossed with a sheepdog from Australia, or it may be descended directly from a dog from Down Under, and some people believe it carries the blood of the Australian wild dog, the dingo.

Aussies are herding dogs, and very skilled ones. Even today, they work in the United States as cattle dogs.

Tough, energetic, and highly trainable, they require a lot of physical activity.

These observant dogs have a knack for being in tune with their owners' thoughts, and they are deeply affectionate toward their owners and those they perceive as being part of the owners' families. And, although they are highly territorial,

Australian shepherds bark sparingly, though many of them like to "chat."

Use a hard brush for grooming, and note that their coats tend to form clumps of hair (which they may try to eat when they shed, so clean up carefully).

Bearded Collie

Place of origin: United Kingdom

54 days

54 days

Bearded collie puppies have distinct coat colors that lighten at about 6 months and set about 1 year later, except for those with solid black coats, and their hair eventually covers their large eyes.

These natives of the Scottish Highlands, a vast, cold wilderness often rainy and thick with fog, are named for their long, beardlike muzzle hair. Beardies—also called highland collies and hairy mountain dogs—though of uncertain origin and lineage, have worked as sheepdogs there for about 2,000 years.

The sheepherding instinct of the gentle, friendly, and increasingly popular beardie is still at work. "When my family goes for a walk with our dogs and someone drops behind," says one owner with a smile, "the beardie becomes nervous and frustrated." Another owner comments, "I've seen a beardie trying to herd other dogs in the dog run."

"They will never be all over you," yet another owner says. "They are very sensitive to the owner's feelings and express tenderness in a casual manner. They are dogs that are never in your way."

Until they are 12–18 months old, their "puppy coat" is still very soft and tends to tangle easily, requiring careful brushing; their coat acquires its distinct roughness only at about 3 years.

Size: [male] Height: 21–22 inches; weight: about 49 pounds
[female] Height: 20–21 inches; weight: 49 pounds

Coat: Harsh; undercoat is soft and dense. Long muzzle fur resembles a beard. Colors include slate, gray, brownish fawn, and white with black or orange markings; some have a blaze or a collar.

AKC/Herding; KC/Pastoral

54 days

Belgian Sheepdog

Place of origin: Belgium

In 1891, Belgian veterinary professor Adolphe Reul divided Belgian shepherd dogs by coat color and quality; otherwise, the standards are identical. Some kennel clubs recognize them as separate breeds; others categorize them as one breed with four types (including the less-common wirehaired Laekenois). Crossbreeding between types is now prohibited.

The dogs of the long-haired Groenendael breed, named after a castle near Brussels, are alert and agile, with a marked wariness.

(continued on page 20)

27 days (Groenendael)

27 days (Groenendael)

27 days (Groenendael)

27 days (Groenendael)

The masked, short-coated Malinois breed, very similar to a German shepherd dog, derives from the Malines area in Belgium. The Tervuren breed, resembling a long-haired German shepherd dog and named for a Brussels suburb, is derived from crossbreeding the others. Its beautiful coat, much softer to the touch than it appears, takes a few years to grow fully.

Belgian shepherd dogs handle vigorous training well and work actively as sheepdogs, sled dogs, and police and rescue dogs. All require a lot of exercise.

The long-haired types must be brushed very carefully during the shedding period.

Malinois

80 days (Malinois)

Malinois

80 days (Malinois)

Size: [male] Height: 24–26 inches; weight: 71–80 pounds
[female] Height: 22–24 inches; weight: 71–80 pounds

Coat: Long (Groenendael), short (Malinois), long and straight, with dense undercoat (Tervuren). Colors are black (Groenendael), fawn, with black mask (Malinois), varying from fawn to mahogany with black-tipped overcoat, a black mask, and black ears (Tervuren).

Remarks: AKC and KC recognize three breeds: Belgian sheepdog, Belgian Malinois, and Belgian Tervuren (AKC); Belgian shepherd dog (Groenendael), Belgian shepherd dog (Tervuren), and Belgian shepherd dog (Malinois) (KC). Also called *chien de berger* Belge (French, "Belgian sheepdog").

AKC/Herding; KC/Pastoral

Tervuren

140 days (Tervuren)

Border Collie

Place of origin: United Kingdom

40 days

40 days

Size: [male] Height: 20–22 inches; weight: 40–51 pounds
[female] Height: 19–21 inches; weight: 36–44 pounds

Coat: Long, thick, and wavy or slightly curly; undercoat is soft and dense. Colors include black, tan and white, and blue merle. (No restriction of color, except never predominantly white.)

AKC/Herding; KC/Pastoral

By 1–2 months, Border collie puppies will have both distinct characters and the typical coat of their breed. Dogs of this breed tend to push themselves to meet their owners' expectations, so people should take care not to demand excessive exercise during their growing years. Also, Border collies are highly sensitive to moving objects and will pursue them, so they must be carefully trained while they are still very young.

This breed, once called the Scottish collie, or simply the collie (perhaps, like the name for the collie breed, from a word for "sooty"), was developed in the area bordering England and Scotland, hence its name. It is considered the most capable of all sheepdogs, with a natural ability to control sheep, and ranchers rave about it and claim one dog can do the work of several ranch hands.

Restless and best kept occupied, Border collies have remarkably long attention spans, are highly motivated, and take pleasure in accomplishing tasks, thus their reputations as workaholics. Because of their natural ability, Border collies do not differentiate between playing and accomplishing tasks, which makes them ideal for people who need canine companions that can accomplish specific goals. One owner says that training them is like playing a game of wits.

80 days

Bouvier des Flandres

Countries of origin: France, Belgium, and the Netherlands (specifically, the region of Flanders)

30 days

Bouvier des Flandres puppies may take more than 2 years to mature. And, as one owner says, "They are very independent. Even if the mother is not nearby, they sleep at ease. They are low maintenance."

The gentle, peaceful, and graceful Bouvier des Flandres originally lived and worked as cattle dogs (their name is French for "cattle dog of Flanders")

and pack dogs in the Flanders (Flandre) region in northern Europe. They have also been known as *Vuilbaard* (Dutch, "dirty whiskers"), *Koehond* (Dutch, "cattle dog"), *boeuf* (French, "beef," meaning "cattle-driving dog"), and *chien de vacher* (French, "shepherd's dog"). Brave and highly trainable, they were used as military and spy dogs and for smuggling. Today, after rebounding

from near extinction after World War I, they work as police dogs and Seeing Eye dogs.

Patorashie, a canine character in the legendary children's story *A Dog of Flanders,* by French author Ouida, is a Bouvier des Flandres. This story of friendship between a boy and a dog is also a tragic tale of trust, betrayal, and forgiveness. Today, statues of the

Size: [male] Height: 25–28 inches; weight: 76–96 pounds
[female] Height: 24–27 inches; weight: 76–96 pounds

Coat: Coarse, harsh, and dense, with eyebrows, a beard, and whiskers. Color ranges from black to fawn, plus salt-and-pepper.

Remarks: Kennel clubs require docked tail (tailless is also acceptable) and cropped ears.

AKC/Herding; KC/Working

30 days

30 days

30 days

two friends stand by the Hoboken Tourism Center in Belgium.

The large-boned, solid, reliable Bouvier des Flandres are calm and very faithful to their owners, but they are wary of other people, though they don't bark without reason. "They don't flirt with people," one owner says. "They never come running to you and lick your face. They behave like big cats." This breed is also intelligent and athletic.

Despite its rough appearance, the coat of the Bouvier des Flandres tangles easily and requires thorough grooming with a metal brush and comb. Also, their ears should be cleaned regularly.

Cardigan Welsh Corgi

Place of origin: United Kingdom

70 days

70 days

70 days

In the small corgi family, the one with the distinctive tail, which sways as it walks, and the flowing coat is the Cardigan. (This breed and its cousin, the Pembroke, otherwise look alike, though their ancestral breeds are different.) Otherwise, another unusual feature is the "corgi carpet," in which they lie flat on their stomachs with their short legs and tail splayed.

This breed is said to have come to the Welsh county of Cardiganshire from central Europe with the Celts more than 3,000 years ago. The Welsh found their short stature, courage, and alertness to be advantageous for working amid cattle. They were also useful as guard dogs and for keeping rodents and small animals under control.

Corgi, originally spelled *Korgi*, is Welsh for "small dog," and they used to be called *Ci Llathaid*, which means "dog by the yard," referring to their

Size: [male] Height: 11–13 inches; weight: 30–39 pounds
[female] Height: 11–13 inches; weight: 24–34 pounds

Coat: Long and harsh; undercoat is soft and dense. Colors include red, sable, fawn, black and tan, and blue merle, with white markings on legs, chest, and neck. (Solid white dogs are disqualified from dog shows.)

Also called: Welsh corgi (Cardigan) (KC)

AKC/Herding; KC/Pastoral

70 days

typical length from the tip of the nose to the end of the tail. King George VI popularized this breed when he acquired a corgi around the time of World War II.

These highly intelligent dogs love to be around people and to be kept busy; a bored corgi will be a stressed corgi, and they should be allowed to run around as much as they like.

Occasional brushing is enough to keep the coat beautiful.

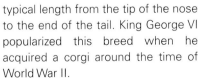

Collie

Place of origin: United Kingdom

40 days

As collie puppies mature, their muzzles grow longer, giving them the distinct collie look, and the coat color gradually becomes more intense.

Collies were long renowned as sheepdogs in Scotland, but their origin and lineage are a bit of a mystery. According to one theory, the sheepdogs that herded "collie" sheep, those with black faces and black legs, themselves came to be called "colly dogs,"

after a word meaning "black with soot." (At the time, many of the sheepdogs were also black. Later, their coat color was primarily tricolor, and blue merle also became more common.) There are now two varieties: the rough (long-haired) and the smooth (short-haired).

In 1860, when Queen Victoria returned from a visit to Scotland, a collie she brought back attracted much attention. Soon after, the sable-

and-white coat color caught on, and the collie gained popularity. The breed later became world famous after publication of the book *Lassie, Come Home,* and subsequent film adaptations and television series. With their slender grace and elegant, long-haired coats, these dogs are loved worldwide. They are intelligent and cheerful and make good household pets as well as excellent guard dogs.

Size: [male] Height: 24–26 inches; weight: 60–76 pounds
[female] Height: 22–24 inches; weight: 51–67 pounds

Coat: Long (rough) or short (smooth). Colors include
sable and white, tricolor (in which black is dominant),
blue merle, or white (with sable or blue-merle markings).

Also called: Scotch collie; rough-coated collie

AKC/Herding; KC/Pastoral

40 days

40 days

These dogs, rather shy and nervous toward strangers but obedient to their families, make good playmates for children as well as ideal household pets if they are trained properly. As they are talented dogs, it is a good idea to challenge them with agility and obedience sports, and they should be kept calm and trained to refrain from barking. Ideally, these dogs should have a big yard where they can run to their heart's content. Otherwise, running and long-distance walking is necessary.

The rough collie loses a lot of hair during the shedding period, thus requiring frequent and thorough brushing.

German Shepherd

Place of origin: Germany

75 days

38 days

Most German shepherd pups, born with black coats, become primarily tan in 2–3 weeks, but their coat color continues to change throughout their lifetime, except for those of dogs with black coats. Their floppy puppy ears will stand erect at 1–2 months.

German shepherd dogs were originally used to herd sheep in the mountainous regions of their place of origin, where they were bred from wolflike sheepdogs. During World War I, they gained recognition for their outstanding performances in delivering medicine and military supplies, watching prisoners, finding wounded soldiers, and delivering messages for the German army.

These brave, calm, active, and very loyal dogs rise to all kinds of challenges and, given the right training, can excel in a variety of tasks. Intelligent and amenable to various types of training, they work as police dogs, military dogs, drug-sniffing dogs, disaster-relief dogs, and See-ing Eye dogs, and in other helpful capacities.

Though they have good qualities, German shepherd dogs can be difficult. It is especially important to sub-ject them to obedience training and to socialize them. The dogs also have a sensitive side, however. According to one owner, "The German shep-herd dog may be more delicate than the Labrador retriever and the golden retriever. When he is taken to a place that is new to him, he bums out for half a day." German shepherd dogs require much exercise, needing a large space in which to run freely, or lots of running on a leash.

Because these dogs shed a lot of hair, they require frequent and thor-ough brushing to maintain their coats.

Size: [male] Height: 24–26 inches; weight: 75–90 pounds
[female] Height: 22–24 inches; weight: 60–70 pounds

Coat: Straight and smooth; undercoat is soft and dense. Colors include black and tan, wolf, black, other solid colors, and black-tipped colors; intense coat colors are desirable.

Also called: Alsatian; *Deutsche Shäferhund* (German, "German shepherd dog") or *Schäferhund* (German, "shepherd dog")

AKC/Herding; KC/Pastoral

Old English Sheepdog

Place of origin: United Kingdom

30 days

At birth, Old English sheepdogs tip the scales at 13–14 ounces—typical for puppies—but their weight will increase 100-fold within a year. Within 6 months, the typical shaggy old English sheepdog hair will hide their lovely round eyes, and, after about 1 year, the fluffy puppy coat gives way to the mature dog's longer, stronger double coat. Even as puppies, they are intelligent and intuitive. One owner says, "When I am busy, he stays quiet. But when he sees I have time to play, he comes to me joyously."

As the name implies, Old English sheepdogs have long worked as herding dogs in the United Kingdom, although they were originally cattle-herding dogs. The characteristic bob-tail (docked tail) is said to have distinguished tax-exempt cattle dogs.

Cheerful and affectionate, Old English sheepdogs are instinctively protective and take good care of their owners, as well as their own puppies and even other dogs. This breed is gentle and quiet but can also be very expressive. When they're happy, for example, they violently wag their hips, and, to show affection, they may lean on you, oblivious of the force of their weight. Also, although their bark is low and forceful (dogs with protruding muzzles, however, tend to bark at a higher pitch), they do not bark unnecessarily.

Very careful and frequent brushing is required so that the hair does not become entangled or felted, and the coat should be clipped in the summer.

30 days

30 days

Size: [male] Height: 24–25 inches; weight: 66–91 pounds
[female] Height: 21–23 inches; weight: 66–91 pounds

Coat: Harsh and shaggy; undercoat is waterproof. Colors include blue, gray, and blue merle, with white markings, or in reverse.

Remarks: Kennel clubs require docked tail.

Also called: Bobtail; bobtailed sheepdog

AKC/Herding; KC/Pastoral

30 days

Pembroke Welsh Corgi

Place of origin: United Kingdom

31 days

28 days

28 days

Size: [male] Height: 10–12 inches; weight: 24–30 pounds
[female] Height: 10–12 inches; weight: 22–28 pounds

Coat: Harsh; undercoat is soft and dense. Colors include red, sable, fawn, and black and tan, with white markings on legs, chest, and neck.

Remarks: A naturally short tail is desirable.

Also called: Welsh corgi (Pembroke) (KC)

AKC/Herding; KC/Pastoral

The Pembroke Welsh corgi puppy's drooping ears prick up within its first 6 months. One owner says, "Most of the puppies are cheerful, but as they grow, they begin to show different characters. Some become gloomy, and shyness and aggressiveness or biting can be corrected by 7 months if they owner deals with them properly."

The Pembroke is distinguished from the Cardigan primarily by its almost nonexistent tail; it must balance with its hind end, producing an endearing wiggling walk. They are slightly smaller than the Cardigan and have a shorter coat, and their triangular ears are slightly sharper looking.

These dogs were originally cattle herders on the farms of Pembrokeshire. Like the Cardigan, the breed gained popularity after the British royal family acquired one during the early 20th century.

This small breed is rather quiet, but its voice is unexpectedly deep and loud. Very intelligent and independent, it is a natural guard dog. Pembrokes need to be trained strictly and given structure and lots of exercise; they enjoy running and are surprisingly fast. Their coat needs to be brushed only occasionally.

95 days

Shetland Sheepdog

Place of origin: United Kingdom

35 days

35 days

35 days

The floppy ears of newborn Shetland sheepdog puppies eventually prick up. (A weight is sometimes used to break the tips of the ears forward.)

The United Kingdom's northernmost islands—the original home of their namesake dogs, located beyond the Orkney Islands, north of Scotland—are known for their harsh natural environment, which has produced unusually small but sturdy flora and fauna, including the famous Shetland ponies.

Shelties, which need lots of exercise, resemble miniature collies, but they have a very long and markedly different heritage. Undersized like the sheep they traditionally herded, they were once called dwarf Scotch shepherds or Shetland collies. Despite their diminutive size, they are excellent sheepdogs, tough and hardworking; they herd sheep by nipping the tips of their charges' legs. One owner says, "They are sensitive to what the owner feels and thinks. They try to read my mind, to pick up what I feel."

The Sheltie's long coat requires a good brushing, especially during the shedding season.

35 days

Size: [male] Height: 13–16 inches; weight: 20 pounds
[female] same

Coat: Long and harsh; undercoat is short, soft, and dense. Fur is feathered around neck, chest, legs, and tail. Colors include sable and white, tricolor (black, white, and tan), and bicolor (black and white).

Also called: Toonie dog (Gaelic/English, "tenant farmer's dog") Peerie ("small, fairylike dog," from Gaelic, "small")

AKC/Herding; KC/Pastoral

American Cocker Spaniel

Place of origin: United States

40 days

The Walt Disney film *Lady and the Tramp* catapulted this breed to fame half a century ago, but it is enjoying a renewed surge in popularity today. The American cocker spaniel was originally a hunting dog, but very few are used for that purpose today. Modified from its British counterpart, the American version is smaller, with a shorter muzzle, a more rounded head, and a pronounced forehead. The coat is more lavish, too, and comes in a wider range of colors.

In the United States, "Cocker spaniel" alone refers to the American breed, while that designation is used for the English cocker spaniel in the United Kingdom, causing some confusion. For clarity, other international kennel clubs add the respective country names.

Members of this attractive, sweet-natured breed are jovial, obedient, and bright. They are also gluttons, though, so, to achieve a balance of glossy coat and healthy skin on the one hand and healthy weight on

Size: [male] Height: about 15 inches; weight: about 29 pounds
[female] Height: about 14 inches; weight: about 27 pounds

Coat: Short on head, medium on body. Feathering on ears, chest, abdomen, and legs. Colors include black, ASCOB ("any solid color other than black"), and parti-color (two or more colors with markings), with tan markings.

Remarks: Kennel clubs require docked tail.

Also called: Cocker spaniel (AKC); spaniel (American cocker) (KC)

AKC/Sporting; KC/Gundog

40 days

87 days

54 days

the other hand, carefully monitor their food intake.

American cocker spaniels look cute in clipped coats but gorgeous in full coats. Their droopy ears also require frequent care; elevate food or restrain the ears during feeding, and consider using a water bottle like those for rodents and rabbits.

Brittany Spaniel

Place of origin: France

Size: [male] Height: 19–20 inches;
weight: about 33 pounds
[female] Height: 18–19 inches;
weight: about 29 pounds

Coat: Flat or wavy. Colors include dark
orange and white, liver (brown) and white,
and (except for AKC) black and white and
tricolor (though black-and-white dogs are
popular among casual American owners);
any color except solid black is accepted
in France.

Remarks: Usually born tailless; kennel
clubs require docked tail, if there is one.

Also called: *Épagneul breton* (French,
"Brittany spaniel"), France Breton, Breton
spaniel (FCI)

AKC/Sporting; KC/Gundog

52 days

52 days

The Brittany spaniel, the only pointing
dog among the spaniels, is much
smaller than pointers and setters, but
its sense of smell is excellent, and it
is second to none on the hunt, hence
its popularity among hunters in the
United States. Its history as a hunting dog dates back to at least the

52 days

17th century, when it was depicted in paintings by French and Dutch artists, including Rembrandt.

Dogs of this expressive, lively, and fast breed are quick learners. They resemble the springer spaniel but have the most slender legs of any spaniel breed. Unlike most spaniels, however, this breed comes not from the United Kingdom but from France. It is also singular in that, unlike other spaniels, its coat is not silky.

Occasional brushing is sufficient, and shampooing is seldom necessary.

Clumber Spaniel

Place of origin: United Kingdom

These puppies may seem dull and clumsy, but they're actually quirky and quick. One owner says, "It seems these puppies would rather be chased than give chase."

Dogs of this gentle and cheerful breed, not particularly speedy but agile enough, were bred as stocky but sharp-nosed bird dogs. Named after Clumber Park in Newcastle in the United Kingdom and popular with the British royal family, they are believed to be related to the alpine spaniel and the basset hound. Their voice is low, and they seldom bark, but adults may snore.

Owners should monitor the dogs' food intake; they are gluttonous and gain weight easily. Also, because of their thick coat, they are sensitive to heat.

Good coat care is required for this breed, which sheds heavily year-round.

110 days

110 days

110 days

Size: [male] Height: about 18 inches; weight: about 76 pounds
[female] Height: about 16 inches; weight: about 66 pounds

Coat: Silky, straight, and dense. Colors include white and lemon and white and orange; lemon or orange markings are on head, muzzle, and legs.

Remarks: Kennel clubs require docked tail.

Also called: Spaniel (Clumber) (KC)

AKC/Sporting; KC/Gundog

English Cocker Spaniel

Place of origin: United Kingdom

35 days

43 days

Size: [male] Height: about 16 inches;
weight: 24–33 pounds
[female] Height: 15–16 inches;
weight: 24–33 pounds

Coat: Silky; short on head and soft and
dense on body. Acceptable colors vary
widely.

Remarks: Kennel clubs require docked tail.

Also called: Spaniel (cocker) (KC)

AKC/Sporting; KC/Gundog

Named in the 17th century, when they were used to hunt woodcocks and moorcocks, they are slightly larger than their American counterparts (which are descended from this breed) and have longer nose bridges. And, although their coats vary less in color than those of American cocker spaniels, they are very silky and elegant. Once known as the land spaniel because it hunted on land rather than in lakes or marshy areas, the breed is closely related to the springer spaniel; it used to be considered merely a smaller variety of that breed.

English cocker spaniels, small but strong and energetic, are quick learners and ideal household dogs, but they need lots of attention. One owner says, "When they are happy, they wag their docked tails as much as they can, or even their entire hips. Their innocent gestures and facial expressions are too cute to explain." Despite their sophisticated appearance, however, they are reliable workers: Many are still used as hunting dogs, and others are employed to sniff out drugs and bombs.

Because of their enormous appetites, their food intake should be monitored carefully.

Daily brushing, especially after a walk, is required to keep their silky coats in good condition, and their ears should be cleaned often.

43 days

35 days

35 days

English Pointer

Place of origin: United Kingdom

29 days

29 days

29 days

29 days

Pointer puppies display their innate hunting ability even while they are still very young; some mimic hunting movements at 2 months.

Along with the English setter, the English pointer, best known of the many pointer breeds, has the longest history of participation in dog shows in the United Kingdom. (The first was held in 1895.) It is a relatively young breed, however, and gained popularity as a hunting dog only at the beginning of the 18th century.

This dog's pendant ears and thin, straight tails, as well as its exceptionally lean body, make it look refined and beautiful. Excellent in tracking, intuition, concentration, endurance, and

Size: [male] Height: 25–28 inches; weight: 50–56 pounds [female] Height: 24–26 inches; weight: 44–50 pounds

Coat: Short, straight, and smooth. Colors include white with reddish-brown, orange, or liver patches, plus (except for KC) solid coats.

Also called: Pointer (AKC, KC)

AKC/Sporting; KC/Gundog

competitiveness, English pointers are archetypal gundogs, built for strength, speed, and endurance.

Because of the English pointer's instinct to chase its quarry, it is important to train this breed to return to you at your command. Some dogs can be impulsive, stubborn, or rough, but early conditioning and thorough obedience training will help them become good household pets. Also, because of their thin coats, they are sensitive to cold.

Their short, stiff coats are very easy to take care of; dirt can be rubbed off with a cloth.

29 days

English Setter

Place of origin: United Kingdom

38 days

38 days

Newborn English setter puppies are generally white, but coat coloring appears gradually, and the colors become more intense at 2–3 months. Even as puppies, these dogs instinctively react quickly to moving objects. The English setter has long had an important role as a bird dog; their popularity coincided with the introduction of hunting guns. This breed, which appeared with English setters in the first dog show in the United Kingdom, in 1895, is said to be derived from spaniel stock.

English setters are known for their stamina and hunting ability, so their natural inclination to track quarry should be controlled early on. They can be good household dogs, but they need lots of training and exercise.

Their elegantly wavy hair requires daily brushing to avoid matting.

Size: [male] Height: 26–27 inches; weight: about 71 pounds
[female] Height: 24–26 inches; weight: about 64 pounds

Coat: Long, straight, and silky. Feathering on ears, chest, legs, and tail. Colors include belton (white with black or brown markings) and tricolor (blue belton—white with black, plus tan).

Remarks: AKC height standard is slightly higher than KC's.

AKC/Sporting; KC/Gundog

38 days

English Springer Spaniel

Place of origin: United Kingdom

Size: [male] Height: about 20 inches; weight: about 49 pounds
[female] same

Coat: Straight and silky. Colors include black and white, liver and white, black plus tan and white, liver plus tan and white, and roan.

Remarks: Kennel clubs require docked tail.

AKC/Sporting; KC/Gundog

In the 19th century, this breed was differentiated from the English cocker spaniel only by its size, but, early in the 1900s, it was recognized by the KC as an independent breed. The name derives from the breed's characteristic springing motion when flushing birds; its large paws give this dog great launching power.

Loyal and gentle by nature, these dogs, like all spaniels, wave their docked tails wildly. They get along well with other dogs and are not territorial, and one owner says of his dog, "He loves to be around children. He lets them do whatever they want."

They also have great stamina, and need to have the run of large yards and to be taken on long walks. However, because of their thick coats, owners should avoid exercising them in hot weather. Also, some English springer spaniels have skin allergies that require a stringent diet and special shampoo.

61 days

61 days

61 days

61 days

Flat-Coated Retriever

Place of origin: United Kingdom

Although flat-coated retriever puppies are adorable little balls of fur, they are especially frolicsome and can often be a handful to care for.

This breed's exact origin is uncertain, though it is believed to be a crossbreed of the Labrador retriever and the Newfoundland. When it first appeared in a dog show in 1859, it was called the wavy-coated retriever because its coat was much more similar to the Labrador's than it is now. Within a few years, however, it had developed the characteristic coat of soft, jet-black fur lying flat against its body. Its other distinguishing feature is its powerful, compact body (it's the smallest retriever).

37 days

37 days

Size: [male] Height: 23–24 inches; weight: 56–78 pounds
[female] Height: 22–23 inches; weight: 49–71 pounds

Coat: Black or liver.

Remarks: AKC stipulates height but not weight; KC and FCI do the opposite.

Also called: Retriever (flat coated) (KC)

AKC/Sporting; KC/Gundog

37 days

37 days

Flat-coated retrievers, cheerful and gentle, are excellent swimmers (their waterproof coats serve as natural thermal swimsuits), and they continue to love to play in water throughout their lives. They make excellent hunting dogs on land and in wet areas, and they require much space and time for exercise.

Occasional brushing will keep this dog's coat clean and shiny; extra care is important during shedding, and their droopy ears need to be cleaned regularly.

Golden Retriever

Place of origin: United Kingdom

45 days

50 days

Though young golden retrievers resemble Labrador puppies, after 4–5 months their light golden fur will grown into long, glossy, water-resistant coats characteristic of the breed. They learn quickly, and training can begin as early as 2 months.

Bred as a hound dog that located and retrieved fallen quarry, golden retrievers are cheerful but rugged water-loving dogs that are popular as household pets and as Seeing Eye dogs and service dogs.

Because genetic hip problems are common in this breed, running on slippery floors, especially with puppies, should be avoided, and owners should take care that their hip joints are not overburdened. They are also more prone to cancer than most other breeds.

To keep their beautiful coats clean and shiny, they should be shampooed after every dirty romp, and brushed often.

45 days

45 days

41 days

Size: [male] Height: 22–24 inches;
weight: 64–76 pounds
[female] Height: 22–23 inches;
weight: 56–64 pounds

Coat: Glossy. Feathering on chest, legs,
and tail. Color is golden; KC and FCI also
accept cream.

Also called: Retriever (golden) (KC)

AKC/Sporting; KC/Gundog

Irish Setter

Place of origin: Ireland

Although the puppy face of the Irish setter does not differ from adult faces as much as those of other breeds, the Irish setter actually matures more slowly than other dogs, taking up to 2–3 years to mature physically and mentally; puppies should not be exposed to strenuous exercise. Also, the vibrant red hue of their coats deepens as they grow.

The Irish setter, dating back to the 15th century, is believed to be the oldest of the setter breeds; it is assumed to be a crossbreed of various setters, pointers, and spaniels. In addition, its ancestors' coats were often red and white, and only in the 1800s was the solid chestnut red introduced.

To distinguish this breed from another setter of Irish origin, called the Irish red and white setter, it is also called the Irish red setter. Dogs of this breed are rejected for breeding if there is any black in their coat; however, small white markings on the neck, throat, and paw tips, though not desirable, are permissible.

Irish setters, cheerful, playful and eager to garner attention, are very emotionally expressive and have colorful personalities to match their long, silky mahogany or chestnut coats. However, they are also especially mischievous and curious, and somewhat demanding; owners must be patient and open-minded enough to entertain this breed's temperament.

This glamorous-looking breed is often mistakenly considered a fashionable dog that is comfortable in urban environments, but in fact Irish setters are active, energetic hounds that need lots of time and space for exercise.

65 days

56

Size: [male] Height: about 26 inches; weight: about 56 pounds
[female] Height: about 24 inches; weight: about 51 pounds

Coat: Mahogany or red, mahogany red, and chestnut red. Feathering on ears, chest, legs, and tail.

Also called: Red setter; Irish red setter (FCI)

AKC/Sporting; KC/Gundog

65 days

Labrador Retriever

Place of origin: United Kingdom

48 days

38 days

48 days

Dogs of this breed settle into their mature characters much earlier than others, and they can be trained to do almost anything. Labrador retrievers love water from puppyhood; their aptitude is matched by their development of short, waterproof coats, otter-like tails, and paddle-shaped paws.

The ancestors of the Labrador retriever were smaller dogs that assisted Newfoundland Island fishermen in picking up fish that had fallen out of nets and retrieving nets that

38 days

had drifted away from the shore. Eventually, they were brought to England, where their retrieving talent was put to use in hunting waterfowl, and the breed was further developed, especially in its size.

Gentle, intelligent, and tenacious, Labrador retrievers are loyal and diligent; they are widely used as police dogs, drug-sniffing dogs, service dogs, and Seeing Eye dogs. Though they're active and need lots of exercise, they make good household pets; clip their nails often, though, to reduce wear and tear indoors.

Like golden retrievers, this breed is prone to genetic hip problems, so they should be kept off of slippery floors. Also, some Labrador retrievers are epileptic. In addition, they gain weight easily and their food intake should be monitored.

Dirt on their coats can be easily removed with a brush and a cloth, and extra brushing will help keep their coat glossy.

Size: [male] Height: 22–25 inches; weight: 60–76 pounds
[female] Height: 21–24 inches; weight: 56–71 pounds

Coat: Short and dense. Colors include black, yellow, and chocolate.

Also called: Retriever (Labrador) (KC)

AKC/Sporting; KC/Gundog

Nova Scotia Duck Tolling Retriever

Place of origin: Canada

55 days

55 days

Puppies' coats grow a darker red with age.

This breed's name derives from the Canadian province and an unusual hunting technique used there: The hunter throws a "tolling stick" for his dog to go after and play with at the water's edge, prompting ducks to respond to the commotion, at which point the hunter shoots them and the dog retrieves them.

The Nova Scotia duck tolling retriever is one of the newest dog breeds in the world; it was recognized by the KC in the 1980s, but the AKC did not acknowledge it until 2003. It is a bright, good-natured, capable dog that is becoming increasingly popular as a household pet. Although they have a relatively high-pitched bark, duck tolling retrievers are generally quiet.

They are also faithful and love to be pampered. An owner says, "If you own this dog along with other dogs or animals, it is difficult to love them equally. But if you want to keep only one dog, this breed may be the best." Duck tolling retrievers, naturally, love to frolic in water, and their need for plenty of exercise should be accommodated.

Occasional brushing is sufficient, though they lose a lot of hair when they shed each year.

Size: [male] Height: about 20 inches; weight: about 51 pounds
[female] same

Coat: Straight and soft; undercoat is dense and softer. Colors include red and variations of orange; white markings on blaze, chest, tip of tail, and paws are permissible.

Also called: American duck retriever; little river duck dog; toller

AKC/Sporting; KC/Gundog

55 days

Weimaraner

Place of origin: Germany

50 days

50 days

50 days

50 days

The blue eyes of newborn weimaraner begin to turn amber at about 3 months. The dogs are very active from a young age and are particularly avid about gnawing.

Once cherished in and around Weimar by German aristocrats who used dogs of this breed to hunt large game such as deer and wild boars, they were long prohibited from leaving the country. They are also adept at hunting birds and smaller animals. Because of the subtle shift in coat color that occurs with changes in lighting conditions, and their swift, quiet movement, they have a mysterious air and were nicknamed "gray ghosts."

50 days

Size: [male] Height: 24–28 inches; weight: 58–78 pounds
[female] Height: 22–26 inches; weight: 56–71 pounds

Coat: Short and glossy. Color ranges from steel gray to silver gray; head and ears are slightly lighter.

Remarks: Kennel clubs require docked tail.

Also called: Weimar pointer

AKC/Sporting; KC/Gundog

Weimaraners are sensitive to noise, and, though they seldom bark, they have a loud, strong call. Also, this breed is not particularly friendly, and they should be socialized while they are still young and should receive thorough obedience training.

This breed is known for its strength and stamina, and weimaraners need a lot of exercise. However, they gain weight easily, so their food intake should be monitored, and they have a tendency to develop calluses, so avoid keeping them on hard floors.

Though weimaraners shed much, their short coats do not require much care; their droopy ears require occasional cleaning.

Afghan Hound

Place of origin: Afghanistan

65 days

40 days

40 days

40 days

Afghan hound puppies take their time maturing, but, by 3–4 years, they resemble gallant princes and elegant princesses.

Afghan hounds, or affies, date back to at least 4000 B.C., on the Sinai Peninsula, and they served the royal families of ancient Egypt and Afghanistan (they were even said to have been on Noah's ark).

Originally, Afghan hounds, swift, sharp eyed, and built for quick turns on rough ground, hunted agile animals such as gazelles through deserts and hilly areas. These intuitive hunters love to run and chase, and they tend to be less responsive when called than most other breeds are, so they need to be trained especially thoroughly.

However, they do not depend on doting attention. One owner says, "After he does what is expected of him, he will go wherever he likes and do whatever he wants. He's never in your way."

The long, silky coats of Afghan hounds require extensive care. Also, their poorly ventilated feathered ears need frequent and careful cleaning.

40 days

Size: [male] Height: about 28 inches; weight: about 60 pounds
[female] Height: about 26 inches; weight: about 51 pounds

Coat: Long and silky. Colors include fawn, golden, cream, red, blue, white, gray, brindle (dark streaks or flecks), and tricolor; all hound colors are permissible.

Also called: Afghan greyhound; *Afghanischer Windhund* (German, "Afghan greyhound" or "Afghan sighthound")

AKC/Hound; KC/Hound

Basenji

Place of origin: Congo

60 days

49 days

60 days

60 days

49 days

At birth, basenjis are more deeply wrinkled than adults of this breed.

Best known for virtually lacking a bark (some occasionally mimic other dogs but never howl or bark idly), these dogs are one of the most primitive of breeds, dating back to ancient Egypt. The name is Swahili for "a small creature in the bush," and the local name in their birthplace is *m'bwa m'kubwa m'bwa wanwitu* ("the dog that leaps"). Known as "dogs of the forest," basenjis were first brought back to Europe in the late 1800s, but not until decades later did any survive distemper, for which they had no natural immunity, or attempts at experimental vaccination.

In their homeland, equipped with wooden bells so they could be tracked, they hunted as retrievers and pointers; they have acute smell and sight. And, although they rarely bark, they communicate eloquently through facial expressions, body language, and noises.

Basenji puppies are very playful and adult dogs relish frequent exercise, but they are not especially friendly and are not ideal household pets; on walks, they tend to follow their owners at a distance. "This is a breed with both the qualities of a cat and those of a dog," one owner points out.

These dogs groom themselves meticulously. One owner says, "He stays away from other dogs' droppings, or steps over them reluctantly. If he accidentally steps in it, he shakes his paw and tries to scrape it off, and he remains disturbed for a long time." Basenjis are also averse to getting wet.

Size: [male] Height: about 17 inches; weight: about 24 pounds
[female] Height: about 16 inches; weight: about 22 pounds

Coat: Short and smooth. Colors include reddish brown and blackish brown; white markings on throat, chest, legs, and tail are permitted.

Also called: Congo dog, Congo bush dog, Congo hunting dog, African barkless dog

AKC/Hound; KC/Hound

Basset Hound

Place of origin: France

Big-boned basset hound puppies, with short legs, baggy coats, pendant ears (which they sometimes trip over), and drowsy eyes, may look awkward, but they're impossible to dislike. Also, though they may look precocious, they grow more slowly than most other breeds and should not be prematurely separated from their mother.

The basset hound (its name derives from *bas,* French for "short" or "low"), built to follow a scent and chase and track down small animals, lacks momentum but has superb endurance.

45 days

45 days

Despite their sad, reluctant appearance, they are affectionate, gentle, and even tempered, and they are social and don't like to be alone. They are a bit stubborn, though, so careful training is essential.

The basset hound's ears are not well ventilated and need to be cleaned inside; because they droop, they need to be cleaned on the outside after walks. Also, an elevated feeding bowl and a water bottle are recommended.

45 days

Size: [male] Height: about 14 inches; weight: about 62 pounds
[female] Height: about 13 inches; weight: about 58 pounds

Coat: Short and smooth. Colors include white and black and tan, tan and white, and black and tan, with silver-gray markings; other hound colorings are acceptable.

AKC/Hound; KC/Hound

Beagle

Place of origin: United Kingdom

38 days

42 days

42 days

Beagle puppies have flapping ears and expressive tails that spin like propellers when they're happy. They look like little black furry balls when they're born, but within a few weeks their color will change to the classic hound colors.

The origin of this breed's name is uncertain; it may be a variant of the Gaelic word *beag* ("small"), or it may have French roots. Beagles, the smallest pack hounds, rely on their acute sense of smell to chase their quarry, and they alert hunters with their high-pitched barks. This trait is likely to be troublesome if a beagle is selected as a household pet, so they must be trained not to bark excessively.

Also, they are independent dogs, and, although they are cheerful and like attention, they aren't especially friendly. In addition, this breed tends to overeat, so their food intake must be monitored so that they avoid acquiring a Snoopy-ish gut.

Their short coats don't shed much and are easy to take care of, but their pendant ears require regular cleaning.

42 days

Size: [male] Height: 13–15 inches; weight: 18–20 pounds
[female] Height: 12–14 inches; weight: 13–16 pounds

Coat: Short and smooth, though hard and dense. Colors include white and black and tan; white and lemon are acceptable.

AKC/Hound; KC/Hound

42 days

Borzoi

Place of origin: Russia

This dignified-looking breed was originally a sight hound used to hunt wolves in the Russian forests; Tolstoy refers to them in his novel *War and Peace*. Before the Russian Revolution, only aristocrats were entitled to keep these dogs, and, afterward, their popularity declined, but dogs owned elsewhere in Europe continued to be bred.

Borzois require a lot of time and space for high-intensity exercise. Also, although they are quietly affectionate, they are sedate dogs that do not exhibit the enthusiasm many other breeds do.

With their gracefully arched backs, deep chests, and long legs, they resemble small Thoroughbred horses from afar when they are running, and their narrow build reduces wind resistance, making them one of the most fleet-footed breeds. That, and their beauty and elegance, combined with intelligence and keen sensitivity, enhances the pleasure of owning one.

Owners must expect to devote much time to grooming, however: Daily brushing of the borzoi's long, wavy, silky coat is a must.

40 days

Size: [male] Height: 28–34 inches; weight: 76–107 pounds
[female] Height: about 26 inches; weight: 60–87 pounds

Coat: Long and silky. All colors are acceptable.

Also called: Russian greyhound, Siberian wolfhound,
barzoi (French, from Russian *borzyi,* "swift")

AKC/Hound; KC/Hound

40 days

Dachshund *(Miniature)*

Place of origin: Germany

Newborn dachshund puppies are normally proportioned; only after 3–4 weeks do their bodies lengthen to their characteristic hotdog or sausage shape, which, thanks to depictions in cartoons, earned this breed the nicknames "hot dog" and "sausage hound." Also, coat colors change at about 2 months; black-and-tan dogs retain their colors, but red coats may lighten and cream ones may change to golden or red.

Sharp-scented dachshunds were originally bred to hunt badgers (the breed name is German for "badger hound"), and the miniature variety was created to hunt rabbits out of their burrows. In their native country, they are called *Zwerg Teckel*.

Long-haired dachshunds are the result of breeding with spaniels; schnauzers and terriers were mated with other dachshunds to produce the wirehaired variety. The "golden ratio" of the dachshund is 2:1; the body length should be twice its height at the shoulder.

(continued on page 76)

(Long-haired)
37 days

(Long-haired) 31 days

(Long-haired) 85 days

(Long-haired)
37 days

(Short-haired)
90 days

(Long-haired) 37 days

(Wirehaired)
66 days

(Long-haired)
53 days

(Long-haired)

42 days

(Wirehaired)

66 days

(Long-haired)

53 days

These dogs are generally jovial, winsome, and a bit self-willed, and, although they are small, they are very brave. Also, because they have an unexpectedly low, loud bark, and they bark often, they should be trained not to do so at random; keeping dachshunds calm and restricting access to windows and doors will also make them less likely to be provoked to bark by outside activity.

In addition, despite their size, they need much exercise, and they enjoy chasing moving objects, as well as digging holes, so these behaviors need to be monitored. They also eat indiscriminately, including their own stool, so their living areas should be kept clear of food and small objects.

Size: [male] Height: 8–10 inches; weight: less than 11 pounds
[female] Height: 7–8 inches; weight: less than 10 pounds

Coat: Smooth, long, or wiry, depending on variety. Colors include red, mahogany red, black and tan, chocolate and tan, dapple, tiger, and brindle; additional acceptable colors for wirehaired dachshunds are wild boar and salt-and-pepper.

AKC/Hound; KC/Hound

(Long-haired)

45 days

(Smooth-haired)

52 days

52 days

52 days

(Long-haired)

45 days

Irish Wolfhound

Place of origin: Ireland

48 days

Surprisingly small (21–30 ounces at birth) compared to their huge parents, Irish wolfhound puppies grow fast, weighing about 8 pounds at 1 month and tripling their weight at 2 months and again a month later. This impressive growth will slow, and they will weigh about 90 pounds by 6 months, although they are not generally fully grown until about 3 years.

Also, their gray faces will turn blacker at about 2 months, and their body color will lighten.

The national dog of Ireland, though not as heavy as the Saint Bernard, is the tallest breed in the world. Its ancestor was a strong breed used to guard cattle and hunt wolves and deer, but when wolves became extinct in the Emerald Isle in the 18th century, the breed declined and very nearly became extinct itself.

However, by crossbreeding Scottish deerhounds, borzois, Great Danes, Great Pyrenees, and Tibetan mastiffs with this other breed, George Graham of Scotland created the modern Irish wolfhound, which continues to slowly increase in size.

48 days

48 days

Dogs of this imposing-looking breed are actually gentle, though, beginning at about 1 year, they should be exercised on a leash.

Coat maintenance is low, but the coat should be brushed frequently enough to pull out dead hairs and make the coat rough and hard; a soft coat tends to gnarl.

Size: [male] Height: 32–34 inches; weight: about 124 pounds
[female] Height: about 30 inches; weight: about 106 pounds

Coat: Hard and rough; long, bristly hairs grow over eyes and under jaw. Colors are gray brindle, red, black, fawn, and white.

AKC/Hound; KC/Hound

Petit Basset Griffon Vendéen

Place of origin: France

73 days

76 days

73 days

Newborn petit basset griffon Vendéen puppies have vivid coat colors that lighten as they mature.

These reasonably fast, capable hound dogs are known for their persistence and stamina rather than their speed, and they were originally used to chase animals into their burrows and drive them out. The French name translates as "small, low, rough-haired (dog of) Vendée" (a place on the west coast of France); the abbreviation PBGV is sometimes used for simplicity. Another variety,

the larger grand basset griffon Vendéen, was bred to hunt hares.

This friendly breed barks loudly but rarely; one owner says, "They are good with other dogs, and people. They are friendly pacifists." However, their food intake should be monitored; they have insatiable appetites and can easily become overweight.

Their protectively hard, rough coat is low maintenance, but those with soft coats should be brushed occasionally to prevent matting.

73 days

73 days

Size: [male] Height: 13–16 inches; weight: 24–36 pounds
[female] same

Coat: Hard and rough; undercoat is short and dense. Colors are black and white, black and tan, white and orange, black with sable markings, and tricolor. Overlaid colors include black with white markings over a fawn base and black over a sable base.

Also called: Basset griffon Vendéen (petit) (KC)

Remarks: Trimmed coats are penalized in dog shows.

AKC/Hound; KC/Hound

Saluki

Place of origin: Egypt

60 days

Saluki puppies seem unusually small compared to their sleek, long-legged parents, but they grow quickly. One owner says, "Compared with whippet puppies, which move very quickly when they play, saluki puppies move as if in slow motion, and their movements seem elegant. But because they are smart and their mischievous tricks are dynamic, you have to keep your eye on them."

Said to be the oldest documented breed, the saluki (its name is Arabic for "of Saluq," an ancient city) is the probable subject of sculptures from the Sumerian empire (7000–6000 B.C.) and was said to be a favorite of Tutankhamen. (Members of this breed, believed by Moslems to be holy, have been excepted from the general Islamic judgment that dogs are unclean animals.) This swift-footed sight hound, with acute hearing as well as keen sight, was used to hunt gazelles and jackals, and its buoyant and elegant running style gives one the impression that it is

Size: [male] Height: 23–28 inches; weight: 44–56 pounds
[female] Height: much smaller than the male; weight: 31–44 pounds

Coat: Smooth and silky. Colors include white, cream, fawn, gold, red, blue and tan, black and tan, and tricolor.

Also called: Persian greyhound, gazelle hound

AKC/Hound; KC/Hound

60 days

flying. Salukis, which need abundant opportunity to run, can accelerate to top speed almost immediately, but owners should note that it is virtually impossible to call them back once they are on the chase.

They are friendly with other household dogs but will shy away from unknown animals; also, their single-minded devotion to their owners can make them seem unfriendly or bashful around other people. In addition, they are sensitive, so obedience training should be especially gentle.

Their short coats need little care, though feathering on their ears and tails should be brushed occasionally.

60 days

Whippet

Place of origin: United Kingdom

30 days

43 days

43 days

Whippet puppies are relatively large, weighing 11 ounces at birth, and only at 1 month or so will they begin to develop their characteristic leggy leanness.

This small race dog (its name probably derives from whip) was creating by breeding smaller greyhounds with terriers and Italian greyhounds, and their strong jaws came in handy for rabbit-chasing races and rat-killing contests.

Although they are born to run and chase and need lots of exercise, they are actually quiet, charming dogs—and they are very social. One owner says, "Adult dogs have a strong sense of camaraderie, and, when they are 3 or 4 years old, they stick together and stop playing and running with dogs in other households. If you have only one whippet, he will be left out."

Their amazingly swift, undulating gait matches the speed of the greyhound, although they accelerate more quickly; it is breathtaking to witness whippets running together at full speed.

43 days

Size: [male] Height: 19–22 inches; weight: about 31 pounds
[female] Height: about 18–21 inches; weight: about 29 pounds

Coat: Hard and glossy. Colors include black, fawn, brindle, and red, plus markings of these colors on a white base (colors are not restricted).

AKC/Hound; KC/Hound

Airedale Terrier

Place of origin: United Kingdom

39 days

50 days

70 days

Newborn Airedale terrier puppies are black, with small brown markings on the tips of their toes and around their eyebrows. As they grow, their hair becomes stiffer and more brown; they acquire adult coats by 6 months.

The Airedale terrier, the largest breed in the group, is fittingly known as the "king of terriers." These intelligent, brave, cheerful, and sensitive dogs make talented hound dogs, police dogs, and military dogs. They also excel at tracking and swimming, which they must have inherited from otterhounds, one of their ancestor dogs.

50 days

However, Airedales are also curious, emotional, vocal, and boisterous; they like to gnaw on things and chase after moving objects, and they remain especially playful and mischievous throughout their life. One owner says, "Whether they are happy or depressed, they react like humans. They are hyper about everything."

Because of their pride and their energetic behavior, however, obedience training may be a challenge. Also, they have strong jaws and large canine teeth, and they can bite and hurt each other while playing.

Stripping should be done about three times a year. Also, daily grooming and regular trimming are required to keep the hair from getting tangled.

70 days

Size: [male] Height: about 23–24 inches; weight: 47–60 pounds
[female] Height: about 22–23 inches; weight: 47–60 pounds

Coat: Rough and wiry. Colors include black or dark colors for body and tan for head, chest, and legs. Markings on head and both sides of ears are dark.

AKC/Terrier; KC/Terrier

Bedlington Terrier

Place of origin: United Kingdom

48 days

75 days

75 days

Newborn Bedlington terrier puppies are black or brown, but, before long, they begin losing their black hair, and their coat color slowly changes to gray or liver. However, they will not begin to resemble their parents until later.

These dogs were miners' pets in Bedlington, a coal town in Northumberland, England, and were used for poaching, catching rats, and dog fighting; despite their dainty appearance, they were known as ruthless fighters.

They were, and are, also excellent hound dogs blessed with the good eyesight and hearing of terriers and a houndlike swiftness at tracking. This energetic breed is believed to carry the blood of the Dandie Dinmont terrier and the otterhound, but its exact origin and lineage are unknown.

Alert and full of fighting spirit, Bedlington terriers are openly wary toward other dogs but obedient to their owners. Gifted with keen senses, they make good guard dogs as well.

The Bedlington terrier has been called a "dog in a lamb's skin" because of the sheeplike trimming the breed has traditionally undergone; professional trimming is required to maintain the coat style. It needs frequent grooming at home as well, too: Use both a comb and a slicker (a wire brush) to care for the unusual combination of hard and soft hair.

75 days

Size: [male] Height: 16–18 inches; weight: 18–22 pounds
[female] Height: 15–17 inches; weight: 16–20 pounds

Coat: Curly and both hard and soft. Colors include blue, blue and tan, liver, liver and tan, liver and sandy, sandy, and sandy and tan.

AKC/Terrier; KC/Terrier

48 days

38 days

Border Terrier

Place of origin: United Kingdom

33 days

90 days

The dark face characteristic of Border terrier puppies becomes lighter as they mature.

Border terriers were once used as hound dogs for foxes that preyed on lambs and as guard dogs in the frontier of Scotland and England, hence their name, though, alternatively, it may derive from when they were teamed up with a breed called the Border foxhound, which tracked foxes before the smaller Border terriers went into their burrows to ferret them out.

Adult dogs have strong jaws and thick, saggy skin, and are known for their beards and their otterlike faces. Among terriers, this breed has rather

Size: [male] Height: 9–11 inches; weight: 13–16 pounds
[female] Height: 8–11 inches; weight: 11–14 pounds

Coat: Dense and wiry; undercoat is short. Colors include red, blue and tan, grizzle (bluish gray) and tan, and wheaten (pale yellow).

AKC/Terrier; KC/Terrier

33 days

long, strong legs developed by running behind hunters on horseback. With their compact, robust bodies, they are powerful and tireless, and they need a lot of exercise. Border terriers get along well with other dogs and are quick learners.

The Border terrier's thick double coat—the hard, wiry hair was developed to provide protection in bushes and burrows—is waterproof and can endure thick fog and downpour.

Daily brushing and regular trimming are essential.

90 days

Bull Terrier

Place of origin: United Kingdom

86 days
(Miniature bull terrier)

(Miniature bull terrier)

86 days (Miniature bull terrier)

Size: [male] Height: 20–22 inches; weight: 44–56 pounds [female] Height: 19–22 inches; weight: about 44 pounds

Coat: Hard and glossy. Colors include white, brindle, brindle and white, black and white, and red and white. (For white dogs, white markings on top of the head are permissible.)

AKC/Terrier; KC/Terrier

90 days (Bull terrier)

(Bull terrier)

MINIATURE BULL TERRIER

Size: [male] Height: about 12 inches;
weight: about 24 pounds; [female] same

Coat: Same as the bull terrier.

Also called: Bull terrier (miniature) (KC)

AKC/Terrier; KC/Terrier

Newborn bull terrier puppies are slender, but this quality is temporary: They soon grow up to be stocky and muscular.

This breed was developed for bullbaiting and bearbaiting in the United Kingdom. Because of their brave yet gentlemanly fighting style, bull terriers were once referred to as "white knights." After these sports were banned, these dogs were bred to be cheerful and friendly, but they still retain a fighting spirit. Comments by owners include, "He likes people, but he is sort of like a spoiled child," and, "He will do what he decides to do. He never forgets what he doesn't like."

True to its appearance, this breed has a strong character, and rigorous training should begin early; also, owners should have enough physical strength and technique to provide serious discipline. One breeder warns, "Never allow them to get too frisky." It is important to take these dogs for long walks, but never let go of the leash, and maintain strict control.

The miniature bull terrier is a different breed, but the only real difference is its size. Standards other than height and weight are the same for both. The miniature bull terrier's nature is a little gentler, and, because it is smaller, it is naturally easier to keep.

Coat care is easy, although despite the dog's tough appearance, its skin is delicate.

90 days
(Bull terrier)

Cairn Terrier

Place of origin: United Kingdom

64 days

64 days

64 days

64 days

64 days

Puppies' coats are sparse and look scraggly compared to those of adults, but they gradually become rich and fluffy. Their coat color will also change; in some cases, it continues to change even on grown dogs. Its drooping ears will normally prick up at 3–4 months.

These bright, alert dogs make good companions for human children; Toto, of *The Wizard of Oz* fame, was a cairn terrier. And, just like him, they are brave and strong willed and will confront much larger opponents without flinching.

The cairn terrier is named for the piles of rocks it rooted through to hunt foxes, which lived in burrows beneath them because they could not dig deeply enough in the poor Scottish soil. The breed, long invaluable for protecting cattle, is believed to be the oldest in the Terrier Group and may be the ancestor of the Scottish terriers. King James I of Scotland offered one of these dogs to the French royal family.

Size: [male] Height: about 10 inches; weight: about 14 pounds
[female] Height: about 10 inches; weight: about 13 pounds

Coat: Rough and long; undercoat is dense. Colors include wheaten, sand, gray, brindle, and colors close to black; any colors except white (AKC), no white, black, or black and tan (KC).

AKC/Terrier; KC/Terrier

Jack Russell Terrier

Place of origin: United Kingdom

62 days

Newborn puppies have very slight variations in markings, but, as they grow older, individual differences such as coat length, hair quality, appearance, and body shape will become more distinct.

The Reverend Jack Russell, who loved fox hunting, developed this intelligent, courageous, tenacious, energetic, and compact breed in pursuit of the ideal hound dog. Their bodies are just the right size to fit in fox burrows, and they have flexible joints, pendant ears, and white coats that keep them from being mistaken for their quarry by hunters.

To control their qualities, one owner says, "Play rough with them, and, while playing with them, teach them who's boss. It is important to start training when they are puppies. Training after they are grown will not work." Another says, "Enjoy their unique temperament rather than thinking that they are unruly."

These persistent chasers tend to rush recklessly after moving objects. Care should be taken that they don't dash out into moving traffic.

The breed's name and standards are in flux. The AKC recently changed the breed name from the Jack Russell terrier to the Parson Russell terrier,

62 days

31 days

31 days

and moved the breed to the Terrier Group from the Miscellaneous Group in April 2003. (Some kennel clubs use the name Parson Jack Russell Terrier.) The KC recognizes only the Parson Russell Terrier, which has longer legs.

Size: Jack Russell terrier [male] Height: 9–11 inches; weight: 11–13 pounds [female] same
Parson Russell terrier [male] Height: 12–14 inches; weight: 11–13 pounds [female] same

Coat: White should be more dominant than black, brown, and tan markings.

Remarks: Kennel clubs consider docked tail optional.

AKC/Terrier; KC/Unrecognized (KC recognizes Parson Russell Terrier)

31 days

Kerry Blue Terrier

Place of origin: Ireland

60 days

60 days

60 days

60 days

Newborn Kerry blue puppies are as black as ink, but, as they mature, their coats usually fade to a charcoal gray and then become an attractive shaggy blue; the color seems to settle in at about 18 months. (Occasionally, a dog remains black, which disqualifies it from dog shows.)

This breed, once called the Irish blue terrier, derives its present name from its origins in Kerry, the southwestern province of Ireland. Because of their bravery, they were once called "blue devils," and they make powerful friends but dreaded enemies. As one owner says, "They are loyal to their master. It seems that they have a strong determination to protect the family, including both people and other dogs."

These dogs, with their trademark luxuriant beard and curly blue hair, are intelligent and powerful and can manage almost any type of work.

Size: [male] Height: 18–21 inches; weight: 33–40 pounds
[female] Height: 17–20 inches; weight: 29–36 pounds

Coat: Soft and somewhat long. Colors include silver blue and smoke blue.

Remarks: Kennel clubs require docked tail; trimming is necessary.

Also called: Irish blue terrier

AKC/Terrier; KC/Terrier

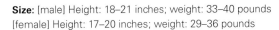

60 days

60 days

They require a good deal of walking, playing, and interaction. They are amphibious, hunting otters in the water as well as rabbits and rats on land, and are excellent cattle dogs that have excelled at herding sheep and pigs as well. Recognized for their talent and good work attitude, some even work as police dogs and guard dogs in the United Kingdom.

This terrier has a topcoat but no undercoat, which is rare for breeds in this group; because of this characteristic, they have very little odor or hair loss.

The coat is easy to maintain, but it requires daily brushing, and their beards need combing.

Lakeland Terrier

Place of origin: United Kingdom

45 days

The colorful coat of a Lakeland terrier puppy continues to lighten until about 4 months. At that point, its soft hair should be stripped to produce a wiry coat; soft hair on the eyebrows and legs is desirable, so those areas should not be stripped.

The Lakie's ancestors were dogs that were good at tracking down foxes living in burrows in the Lake District of northern England as far back as several hundred years ago; their narrow chests permitted them to crawl into small foxholes after their quarry.

These intelligent, energetic, and playful dogs are good observers, but one bad habit left over from their foxhunting days is a penchant for digging holes.

The more care devoted to the coat, the more attractive and wiry it will become; trimming is also necessary. The Lakeland terrier's rich, wiry beard may get in the way while eating, but it is easily cleaned with a cloth.

45 days

Size: [male] Height: 14–15 inches; weight: about 18 pounds
[female] Height: about 14 inches; weight: about 17 pounds

Coat: Wiry; undercoat is soft; featherings on muzzle and legs.
Colors include blue, black, red, wheaten, liver, and blue and tan.

Remarks: Kennel clubs require docked tail.

AKC/Terrier; KC/Terrier

Miniature Schnauzer

Place of origin: Germany

36 days

36 days

40 days

Most terrier breeds originated in the United Kingdom as hound dogs that hunted vermin, such as foxes, that preyed on farm animals. However, the miniature schnauzer was developed to guard farm stables and catch rats in Germany.

These dogs are very distinctive looking, with their trademark long, soft whiskers (*Schnauzer* is German for "whiskers"), bushy eyebrows that give them a wise demeanor, and long featherings on their legs.

The miniature schnauzer, based on the standard schnauzer and bred with the Affenpinscher and the poodle, is quite different from the standard and giant breeds, which are introduced in the Working Group section of this book.

Alert, intelligent, and fearless, miniature schnauzers are popular for their serious looks and likable character. Also, because they are naturally very cautious and bark a lot, they make good guard dogs.

They are strong and quick to learn but easy to keep, but they can be stubborn and tend to be wary of other dogs. They should be given work to do and given free rein to exercise, but, because of their tendency to bark, they should not be overstimulated. Also, they gain weight easily, so their food intake should be monitored.

Their coat needs daily brushing and combing, and occasional plucking is required to remove excess hair.

Size: [male] Height: 12–14 inches; weight: 11–18 pounds
[female] same

Coat: Hard and wiry; undercoat is soft. Colors include salt-and-pepper, black and silver, and black.

Remarks: Kennel clubs require docked tail; AKC requires cropped ears (KC does not accept cropping).

Also called: *Zwergschnauzer* (German, "small schnauzer")

AKC/Terrier; KC/Terrier

40 days

40 days

Norfolk Terrier

Place of origin: United Kingdom

60 days

This breed, once considered a variation of the Norwich terrier, was originally called the drop-ear Norwich terrier. However, in 1964, the KC created an independent breed, and the AKC recognized it in 1979. (Their hometown is Norwich, in Norfolk in eastern England.)

In the 1880s, Cambridge University students kept small terriers as ratters. One of them, named Rags, is said to be the ancestor dog of the two breeds. The Norfolk terrier was also called the Trumpington terrier, after a street in Cambridge.

The primary difference between the breeds is their ears. The Norfolk terrier has drop ears set well apart from each other, with rounded tips. Owners of prick-eared puppies often encourage their ears to drop by stroking them, taping them down, or weighting them.

Intelligent and delightful, these dogs make great household pets, but they are full of energy and need lots

60 days

45 days

of exercise. They are also very adventurous and like to dig holes, so they need to be watched carefully. And, though they are the shortest of the Terrier Group, these dogs have stocky bodies and strong legs.

Size: [male] Height: about 10 inches; weight: 11–13 pounds
[female] Height: 9–10 inches; weight: 10–12 pounds

Coat: Wiry. Colors include red, wheaten, grizzle, and black and tan.

Remarks: Kennel clubs require docked tail; trimming is necessary.

AKC/Terrier; KC/Terrier

Scottish Terrier

Place of origin: United Kingdom

45 days

45 days

45 days

45 days

Scottish terrier puppies are self-confident adventurers that start scurrying around as soon as they learn to walk. And, in spite of their short legs, they move fast. One owner says, "Unlike other breeds, they don't play together. They are independent puppies." They are also aggressive, so they should socialize with people and other dogs from a young age.

This breed, originally from Aberdeen, Scotland, is nicknamed the Scottie and was once called the Aberdeen terrier. Originally bred as hound dogs for small animals such as foxes, badgers, and weasels that preyed on farm animals, the Scottie has short legs that are convenient for crawling into burrows. Because of their sharp senses, they made, and make, good guard dogs as well, though they should be trained not to bark unnecessarily.

45 days

Training in general is very important for this breed, though overly strict methods will make them stubborn. Owners must be flexible and accepting of the Scottie's strong character. Also, they are curious and are enthusiastic hole diggers.

Size: [male] Height: 10–11 inches; weight: 19–22 pounds
[female] Height: 10–11 inches; weight: 18–21 pounds

Coat: Hard and wiry; undercoat is soft and dense. Colors include black, brindle, gray, and wheaten; a small white marking on the chest is permissible.

AKC/Terrier; KC/Terrier

Sealyham Terrier

Place of origin: United Kingdom

46 days

46 days

89 days

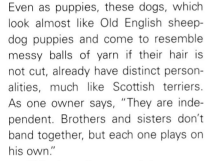

Even as puppies, these dogs, which look almost like Old English sheepdog puppies and come to resemble messy balls of yarn if their hair is not cut, already have distinct personalities, much like Scottish terriers. As one owner says, "They are independent. Brothers and sisters don't band together, but each one plays on his own."

This breed, created by crossbreeding bull, Staffordshire bull, West Highland white, and Dandie Dinmont terriers, as well as corgis, was named after Sealyham in southwestern Wales, where it was developed. In concert with packs of otterhounds, Sealyham terriers worked as hound dogs, chasing down otters and badgers; they were bred to have whitish coats to avoid being mistaken for their quarry.

These fearless dogs, which serve well as guard dogs, bark loudly for their size but will not do so without reason. Many people are impressed by their cuddly appearance, dominated by their elegant beards and drop ears, but may be surprised by their proud, intelligent temperament.

89 days

Tough and energetic, they require plenty of exercise, but their food intake must be monitored, as they gain weight easily.

Maintaining proper and regular coat care is indispensable. As with other wirehaired terriers, their soft hair must be stripped and the coat should be combed.

46 days

Size: [male] Height: about 11 inches; weight: about 20 pounds
[female] Height: about 10 inches; weight: about 18 pounds

Coat: Hard and wiry; undercoat is soft and dense. Colors include white and white and lemon; tan markings on the head and ears are permissible.

Remarks: Kennel clubs require docked tail.

AKC/Terrier; KC/Terrier

109

Soft-Coated Wheaten Terrier

Place of origin: Ireland

88 days

The muzzles and lower faces of newborn soft-coated wheaten terrier puppies are black, but they will gradually lighten, and by 2 years the black markings will disappear, except for the nose and the tips of the ears. Honey-coated dogs tend to keep their masks until they are more than 1 year old, but the mask on true wheaten-coated dogs fades within 2–3 months.

Dogs of this cheerful, friendly, and intelligent breed, ancestors of the Kerry blue terrier and the Irish (red) terrier, once worked as sheepdogs, guard

60 days

20 days

88 days

dogs, and dogs used to control foxes and other animals in northwestern Ireland. They require a lot of attention and exercise.

The silky double coat of this breed, which is less wavy than the Kerry blue terrier's, tends to get tangled and requires frequent brushing and combing.

Size: [male] Height: 18 inches or less; weight: 40 pounds or less
[female] Height: 18 inches or less; weight: 33 pounds or less

Coat: Silky and wavy or curly. Colors include wheaten and honey.

Remarks: Kennel clubs require docked tail. Trimmed for AKC dog shows (but too much trimming will result in penalties); not normally trimmed for KC dog shows.

Also called: Irish wheaten terrier; Irish soft-coated wheaten terrier (FCI)

AKC/Terrier; KC/Terrier

60 days

Welsh Terrier

Place of origin: United Kingdom

54 days

54 days

54 days

The inky black coat color on newborn puppies assumes a blanket marking, which makes these dogs look like they are carrying saddles, after about 3–4 months.

If the Airedale terrier is the king of terriers, the much smaller Welsh terrier is the prince of the family. Once called Old English terriers or black-and-tan wirehaired terriers, these dogs have a long history of hunting foxes, badgers, and otters in Wales. Cautious and brave, they make very good guard dogs.

These dogs are intelligent and well behaved, and they like to be around people; they will not thrive if left on their own.

Careful brushing of their wire-haired double coat, and occasional clipping, is sufficient for household pets.

54 days

54 days

Size: [male] Height: about 15 inches; weight: about 20 pounds
[female] Height: about 14 inches; weight: about 18 pounds

Coat: Wiry; undercoat is soft and dense. Color is tan, with black on back, or dark grizzle with tan.

AKC/Terrier; KC/Terrier

54 days

West Highland White Terrier

Place of origin: United Kingdom

43 days

43 days

43 days

Newborn Westie puppies are white from head to toe, with pink noses and footpads. Within 3–4 days, their noses and the footpads start getting mole-size black spots that increase until those body parts are all black. Their folded ears will prick up in 2–3 months. From puppyhood, they are geniuses at playing. One owner says, "If he finds one little stick, he can make a fun toy out of it. If he has a toy, he plays well by himself. He plays well with other dogs, too. He finds a good playmate in his mother, and they play together for a long time."

Size: [male] Height: about 11 inches;
weight: 20 pounds or less
[female] Height: about 10 inches;
weight: 18 pounds or less

Coat: Wiry; color is white.

AKC/Terrier; KC/Terrier

43 days

43 days

This cheerful but tough and strong-willed breed, named after its homeland in Scotland, was developed from white cairn terriers, which were originally considered weak and cowardly and were commonly weeded out. But then white cairn terriers were bred to make small terriers to hunt small animals. Sensitive to sound, they make good guard dogs, and they need lots of exercise.

Crossbreeding this breed with the cairn terrier was practiced and accepted for a long time, but, since 1917, the AKC has not recognized registration of these crossbred puppies.

Their rough double coat looks soft, but it is coarse and made for the outdoors. Stripping dead hair and trimming are frequently required.

Wire Fox Terrier

Place of origin: United Kingdom

50 days

45 days

45 days

The black markings on wire fox terrier puppies' faces eventually turn brown and then tan, settling by about 2 months; the only permanent black is on their backs. Compared to other breeds, newborn puppies of this breed have rather long faces.

These dogs were originally bred for foxhunting, tracking their quarry, sniffing out their burrows, and killing it. Later, they were trained to drive the foxes out of their burrows for hunters to kill.

The breed has a long history, but its exact origin is uncertain. Only in the 18th century were they called fox terriers. Their coat color resembled that of foxes, so the current colors were developed to prevent mistaken identity.

These feisty, impulsive dogs track and catch quarry instinctively. One owner says, "A Scottish terrier takes action after the quarry approaches, but a fox terrier just runs as soon as he sees moving objects in the distance." They need a lot of exercise, but they must be trained carefully so that they do not endanger themselves in traffic. Also, their tendency to bark makes them good guard dogs, but they should be trained not to bark unnecessarily.

Frequent brushing and combing are necessary.

45 days

45 days

Size: [male] Height: 16 inches or less; weight: 15–20 pounds
[female] Height: 14 inches or less; weight: 13–18 pounds

Coat: Wiry; undercoat is soft and dense. Color is predominantly white, with black and tan markings; brindle, liver, and red markings are undesirable.

Remarks: Kennel clubs require docked tail.

Also called: Fox terrier (wire) (KC)

AKC/Terrier; KC/Terrier

45 days

Brussels Griffon

Place of origin: Belgium

The Brussels griffon has two types: smooth coated, which is short-haired, and rough coated, which is wire-haired. When dogs of the two varieties mate, puppies may turn out rough coated or smooth coated. At birth, they cannot be distinguished, but, soon, the rough-coated puppies will develop soft whiskers.

This distinctive-looking farm dog, called "the griffon of the stable" in Belgium, was originally useful for catching rats. The breed was developed by mixing the Affenpinscher, known for its simian appearance, with Belgian dogs, and, through cross-breeding with pugs, their muzzles became shorter. Like the pug and other breeds with flat noses, these dogs snore loudly.

"They are basically lovely and friendly dogs," one owner says. "They are also easy to keep, because they are robust."

The smooth-coat type doesn't require any special care except brushing, but the rough-coat type requires stripping to keep the coat hard and must be groomed every 3 months or so using hair clippers.

60 days

60 days

(Smooth)

(Rough)

Size: [male] Height: about 8 inches; weight: 8–10 pounds
[female] same

Coat: Wiry or short, depending on variety. Colors include reddish tones and solid black.

Remarks: Kennel clubs require docked tail and cropped ears.

Also called: *Griffon bruxellois* (French, "Brussels griffon") (KC); black longhaired dogs: *griffon Belge* (French, "Belgian griffon"), smooth-haired dogs: *petit brabançon* (French, "small Brabant griffon") (FCI)

AKC/Toy; KC/Toy

60 days

Cavalier King Charles Spaniel

Place of origin: United Kingdom

35 days

50 days

Size: [male] Height: 12–14 inches; weight: 10–19 pounds [female] same

Coat: Long and silky, with feathering on ears, chest, and legs. Colors include black and tan, ruby (red), blenheim (red and white) and Prince Charles (tricolor).

Remarks: Kennel clubs consider docked tail optional.

AKC/Toy; KC/Toy

50 days

35 days

Cavalier King Charles spaniels, or cavs, developed from the King Charles spaniel (which, as the name indicates, won the special favor of Charles II), were favorite pets of the British royal family for more than 300 years.

In the 1920s an American who was impressed by King Charles spaniels depicted in old paintings went to England, hoping to see the real dogs, but the breed had developed into small, flat-nosed dogs with grumpy expressions. However, noticing that longer-muzzled puppies were occasionally born, he developed the cavalier King Charles spaniel from these throwbacks. This breed is also slightly larger than the earlier breed, and it was developed to be more of an outdoor dog than its coddled predecessor.

Though cavs are very popular in the United Kingdom, the breed is not as well known in the United States and was only recently recognized by the AKC.

True to the swashbuckling name, dogs of this breed have adventurous spirits, and, because they are descended from hunting dogs, their wariness makes them ideal guard dogs. They are also sweet natured and obedient, however, and they get along very well with people, including children, as well as other dogs.

Their long coats and the featherings of their pendant ears need to be combed carefully, and other parts require brushing.

Chihuahua

Place of origin: Mexico

(Smooth-haired)

55 days

(Long-haired)

60 days

(Smooth-haired)

(Long-haired)

33 days

29 days

(Long-haired)
52 days

(Smooth-
haired)
55 days

(Long-haired)
59 days

(Long-haired)
56 days

Newborn Chihuahua puppies, from the smallest breed in the world (though the smallest individual dog on record is a Yorkshire terrier), look just like mice, weighing only 2–3 ounces.

This breed is said to have been discovered by an American in the state of Chihuahua in Mexico, but many theories about its origins exist, including that it is a descendant of the *techichi,* the dogs of the Aztecs.

In spite of their diminutive size, Chihuahuas are brave, self-conscious, and curious and will not shy way from larger dogs, and they will bravely confront prowlers, attacking their ankles and heels. One owner, who also keeps a Tosa, one of a large Japanese breed, says, "The big Tosa is trained not to bark, so the Chihuahua is our watch dog." Given their small bodies, their barks are relatively quiet.

"They like to play with and be around people," another owner says. "They sometimes even think of people as their toys." If overprotected, however, they may become difficult to handle.

There are two types of coat: smooth-haired and long-haired. The smooth-haired, with its short coat, may be more sensitive to cold. As one owner says, "When it's too cold, he loses his appetite."

Basically, these are robust dogs, but recent careless breeding to meet increased demand has resulted in deteriorated bone structure of their skulls, which makes them vulnerable to physical impact. One owner says, "One died by hitting his head on the corner of a box of tissues. When I patted another on the head, he had a concussion and died." Also, their fragile legs break easily, and, because their windpipes are small, they do not tolerate heat very well.

In addition, hypoglycemic comas caused by hunger can occur, especially during weaning.

Size: [male] Height: about 5 inches; weight: 2–4 pounds; [female] same

Coat: Smooth or long. Colors include fawn, blue, chocolate, and black.

AKC/Toy; KC/Toy

43 days (Long-haired) 43 days

(Smooth-haired)

52 days

(Long-haired) 59 days

(Long-haired) 56 days

(Long-haired) 52 days

(Long-haired) 54 days

(Long-haired) 55 days

Chinese Crested

Places of origin: Central and South America; Africa

180 days

Newborn Chinese crested puppies of the more common "hairless" variety are born with hair on the head and toes, and the less well-known powder-puff type is covered with short hair. As they grow, their hair becomes longer and their bodies slimmer, and they will develop skin markings that will remain visible on the hairless. As early as 1 month, puppies of this breed are already walking briskly and even jumping.

This breed is said to have been developed by the Chinese, who miniaturized African hairless dogs, but some people believe they are descended from hairless dogs raised for food by the Aztecs in Mexico, and that the name refers merely to the resemblance of their groomed hair to a traditional Chinese queue.

The enigmatic aura of the hairless Chinese crested is enhanced by its bare skin and the soft featherings on the head, tail tip, and toes. Although these dogs are intelligent, friendly and affectionate, they are wary of strangers.

51 days

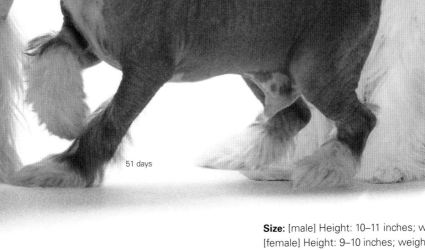

The mating of two hairless or a hairless with a powder puff will produce puppies of both types, but only powder-puff puppies are produced from two powder puffs. Also, mortality rates are high among puppies born from two hairless dogs, and these puppies are sometimes born with a few teeth missing.

The bare skin of the hairless type, though stronger than that of the powder-puff variety, is warm and soft, and has a slightly sticky feeling.

Though the hairless does not require coat care, its skin is vulnerable to strong sunlight, dryness, and cold and can be soothed with cream or baby oil. Powder-puff dogs require brushing.

51 days

51 days

135 days

Size: [male] Height: 10–11 inches; weight: about 16 pounds [female] Height: 9–10 inches; weight: about 13 pounds

Coat: Hairless (except for head, tail tip, and toes) or powder puff. Colors are solid or with markings; any colors are permissible, although the darker the skin color, the better.

Remarks: Tail has feathering and is carried over back.

AKC/Toy; KC/Toy

Italian Greyhound

Place of origin: Italy

Size: [male] Height: 13–15 inches;
weight: 6–10 pounds
[female] same

Coat: Short and glossy. Colors include fawn, red, gray, blue, cream, and white; may have white markings, too, but black and tan, blue and tan, and brindle markings are not permissible.

Also called: *Piccolo levriero Italiano* (Italian, "little Italian greyhound")

AKC/Toy; KC/Toy

50 days

Even when Italian greyhound puppies are small, they love to run. "Once they start running, they don't stop," one owner says. Another owner comments, "Puppies are active, hasty, and shy. They love people but behave like spoiled children."

This old breed, loved by the ancient Egyptians and Greeks as well as by Roman aristocrats, often appears in old European paintings.

About the size of a large cat, the Italian greyhound, or IG, with its dainty and refined manner, wet-looking round eyes, and streamlined bodies, looks remarkably small and frail.

Owners of these dogs can expect to be criticized about their skinny dogs, but Italian greyhounds are all muscle. Puppies and adults alike can hop and jump without a running start and are even known to leap into their owners' arms. Since they are not afraid of heights, however, owners must be careful about the dogs jumping off the furniture or trying to leap over fences. They settle down in adulthood, however, and remain receptive to learning.

Because of their short coats and negligible body fat, they are sensitive to cold.

50 days

50 days

50 days

50 days

Japanese Chin

Place of origin: Japan

Toy Group

58 days

58 days

The Japanese chin has a long heritage as a goodwill ambassador: Asian monarchs exchanged them as gifts, and Commodore Matthew Perry brought one to England's Queen Victoria after his ground-breaking visit to Japan in 1853. During Japan's Edo era (1603–1868), they often appeared in paintings alongside beautiful women, and the 17th-century shogun Tsunayoshi favored the breed.

This ideal breed is gentle, friendly, and obedient, and is easily toilet trained (and trained in general) and nearly free of the typical dog odor. In addition, it rarely barks, and it likes to be held. One owner says, "They are so quiet, our neighbors couldn't believe that we had dogs."

Their large, wide-set eyes protrude and are somewhat vulnerable, so care should be taken not to hurt

58 days

their eyes. Also, be vigilant about eye diseases; otherwise, this is a very healthy breed.

Though Japanese chins are long-haired and shedding is common, grooming is easy because they lack a thick undercoat. Brushing and combing prevents hair balls and keeps their coats shiny. Also, their droopy ears need to be kept clean.

Size: [male] Height: about 9 inches; weight: about 7 pounds
[female] same

Coat: Long, silky, and glossy; feathering around jaws and on ears, legs, and tail. Color is white base with black or red markings; symmetrical markings and hair between the toes are desirable.

Also called: Japanese spaniel

AKC/Toy; KC/Toy

Maltese

Place of origin: Malta

Newborn Maltese puppies, which resemble soft, white balls of yarn, may initially have fawn-colored hair around their ears, but it gradually fades until the entire body is covered in a pure white coat, though their noses and eye rims become darker as they mature.

This breed, called by various names, including the Maltese terrier, the Maltese spaniel, the Maltese

62 days

62 days

62 days

62 days

Size: [male] Height: 8–10 inches; weight: 4–7 pounds
[female] same

Coat: Long, straight, and silky. White is desirable.

Remarks: The tail has long, rich feathering and is raised over the back.

Also called: *Bichon maltiase*

AKC/Toy; KC/Toy

poodle, the *bichon maltiase,* and the Melita dog, is said to have been brought to its Mediterranean island home, a key trading center, by the Phoenicians as far back as 1500 B.C. Some people believe, however, that it is the island of Meleda in the Adriatic Sea, not Malta, where they originated.

In one of Aesop's fables, one of this breed appears as a "white dog of Malta" that accompanies doting sailors on a long voyage. In 15th-century France, they served as lapdogs for noblewomen, and, after Queen Victoria had one ordered from Malta in the late 1800s, the breed, suddenly in high demand, was for a time bought and sold at very high prices.

These intelligent and quick-learning dogs are lively and playful, and, despite their soft bearing and elegant appearance, they are fairly daring. Also, their barks are unexpectedly loud and high pitched.

Their long, silky hair needs frequent care for it to remain snow white. Also, their eyes should be wiped carefully each morning and their mouths cleaned after each meal, and their bottoms should be cleaned after bowel movements.

Manchester Terrier (toy)

Place of origin: United Kingdom

63 days

The ears of toy Manchester terriers droop until about 2 months.

This miniaturized version of the Manchester terrier (considered by the AKC a variety, not a separate breed), once used in rat-killing contests in its city of origin, has "candle flame" ears, intelligent eyes, and a lithe body. There are thumb marks on their forefeet and pencilings on their digits. Small tan points over the eyes resemble eyebrows, and points on their cheeks look like lipstick marks.

Both adults and puppies are excellent jumpers. One owner says, "He was left alone in the house while I was gone, but he sneaked out. When I came home, I found him in the neighbor's yard. He must have jumped over the fence."

These dogs are expressive and good at understanding commands, but they have a stubborn streak. As adults, they become wary toward strangers and other dogs, and they require early obedience training and must be taught not to bark idly. Also, they are sensitive to cold.

Occasional brushing of the velvety coat is sufficient.

63 days

Size: [male] Height: 10–12 inches; weight: 7–11 pounds
[female] same

Coat: Short and glossy. Color is black and tan.

Also called: English toy terrier (black and tan) (KC)

AKC/Terrier; KC/Toy

63 days

63 days

Miniature Pinscher

Place of origin: Germany

This breed, nicknamed the minpin, resembles a small Doberman, but its history goes back farther, and the two breeds do not seem to be related. Its ancestral dog is believed to be the *Klein Pinscher*, from Scandinavia, from which it was miniaturized several hundred years ago.

With slim, lithe bodies, frail legs, and large prick ears, they hop around like little fawns, and they can jump as high as a person's waist. Owners report frequently hearing the comment, "He looks more like Bambi than a dog," and one owner remarks, "I feel like I am keeping a miniature dinosaur."

Dogs of this wary, loudly barking breed are ideal guard dogs, and, though they're not as threatening as the Doberman, they are fast and bold. They must be taught not to bark unnecessarily, and careful training is required.

Miniature pinschers are curious and can easily slip away and jump over fences. One owner says, "He escaped from his cage. After a long search, we couldn't find him, and we gave up. Later, we found him sleeping in the bed."

This short-coated breed is sensitive to cold and has a strong canine odor.

33 days

90 days

90 days

33 days

90 days

Size: [male] Height: 10–13 inches; weight: about 10 pounds
[female] Height: 10–13 inches; weight: about 9 pounds

Coat: Hard and glossy. Colors include red, black and tan, and chocolate and tan, though tan is limited to certain positions.

Remarks: Kennel clubs require docked tail.

Also called: *Zwerg Pinscher* (German, "small terrier"), *Reh Pinscher* (German, "roe-deer terrier")

AKC/Toy; KC/Toy

Papillon

Places of origin: France, Belgium

42 days

Although the pap's ears, which look like big ribbons tied in bows, are droopy at birth, they will stand up in 3–4 weeks, resembling a butterfly (which is what their name means in French). If they have rich feathering, the ears become heavy and take more time to prick up. Newborn puppies often have predominantly black or brown coats rather than white ones, but these colors gradually fade away and white becomes dominant.

These dogs were renowned for winning the favors of the Spanish and French courts; Marie Antoinette and Madame Pompadour were fans of the papillon, and many noblewomen were eager to have their portraits painted alongside one of these dogs. Rubens is said to have owned one.

Papillons with drooping ears, called phalenes (from the French word for "moths"), although recognized as a variation, are said to be the original type. Both varieties can be produced in one litter.

Their trainability is remarkable; along with poodles, these friendly, highly adaptable dogs are widely used in circuses and other entertainment. However, dogs of this strong, healthy, assertive breed are also used as rescue dogs.

As with other especially small dogs, papillons may sometimes faint from low blood glucose when they are hungry, and, despite their strong personalities, they are given to fawning and are hypersensitive to owners' moods.

Their single coat is easy to care for; light brushing is sufficient.

Size: [male] Height: 8–11 inches; weight: about 10 pounds [female] Height: 8–11 inches; weight: about 8 pounds

Coat: Long, silky, and glossy. Color is white, with black or tan markings, or tricolor; featherings on ear tips, chest, and tail.

Remarks: Tail is carried high over the body like a squirrel's.

Also called: Butterfly spaniel, squirrel spaniel, *épagneul nain continental* (French, "continental toy spaniel"); continental toy spaniel (FCI)

AKC/Toy; KC/Toy

60 days

87 days

48 days

Pekingese

Place of origin: China

21 days

As one owner says, "Puppies that are 1–2 months old are completely trusting and let you do whatever you like with them. They just look quietly into your eyes. They are too cute to let go." Another owner comments, "From about 1 month of age, when you hold them, they won't move. With other breeds, if you put puppies on their backs, they immediately will try to upright themselves. Pekingese puppies will stay on their backs with their four legs up in the air and stare at you."

In China, these dogs, said to be descended from the Lhasa apso, were called lion dogs, for their mane-like feathering, and sun dogs, for their long, straight coats. They were also called sleeve dogs, because they are small enough to be carried around in traditional Chinese outfits. A Chinese legend tells that they were the result of crossbreeding a lion with a kind of monkey, and they were believed to be holy.

Since before the time of Christ, the Dalai Lama gave these dogs as gifts to those who held power in China, and they were cherished and never allowed to be taken out of the palace. Over time, the breed was improved on, and these dogs were so valued that anyone who tried to steal one was executed. During the Opium War, however, the Pekingese was introduced to the Western world for the first time.

Contrary to their frail appearance, Pekes are big boned, and females are slightly heavier than males. They don't require much exercise, although they do enjoy walks.

Their long coats must be brushed carefully several times a week, but avoid shampooing; it damages their coats. Instead, use cornstarch or baby powder to remove dirt, and spray them with water to replenish coat moisture. Also, their sensitive protruding eyes tear easily and must be cared for every day.

21 days

Size: [male] Height: about 8 inches;
weight: 7–14 pounds
[female] Height: about 8 inches;
weight: 7–12 pounds

Coat: Rough and straight; undercoat is relatively long and thick; featherings on ears, chest, legs, and tail. Any color except liver or albino is permissible.

Also called: *Peiking kou* (Chinese, "Peking dog")

AKC/Toy; KC/Toy

21 days

Pomeranian

Place of origin: Germany

At about 3–5 months, because their body grows faster than their coat does and their facial hair is oddly short, Pomeranian puppies resemble monkeys. Around this time, the facial hair of puppies with dark faces will begin to fade, leaving dark hair only at the eyebrows, which will lighten in turn. The Pomeranian's coat grows very fast but takes about 2 years before it develops into the full, long coat.

60 days

70 days

65 days

74 days

66 days

66 days

This excitable, high-spirited breed, with its full coat, triangular prick ears, slightly protruding forehead, and elegant tail carried over the back, seems to belong to the spitz family, but it traces back to the Samoyed.

In its place of origin, where more robust breeds such as the Great Dane and the German shepherd dog are preferred, this breed received less attention; it was only when Pomeranians were introduced into England that they became popular, and, when Queen Victoria became a fan, its reputation was assured. (The British named the breed after the region in Germany and Poland where it originated.)

Daily brushing is required to maintain the Pomeranian's gorgeous coat.

37 days

54 days

54 days

59 days

54 days

69 days

Size: [male] Height: about 7 inches; weight: 3–7 pounds
[female] same

Coat: Straight; undercoat is soft and fluffy; long featherings around head, on front of shoulders, and on chest. Colors include red, orange, black, brown, chocolate, cream, beaver, blue, white, wolf sable, orange sable, parti-color, and black tan.

Remarks: Kennel clubs require tail to be carried over back.

Also called: *Zwerg Spitz* (German, "small spitz")

AKC/Toy; KC/Toy

Pug

Place of origin: China

35 days

Before pugs were introduced to Europe by the East India Company, they had long lived in China, where they were called *ba guo* ("dogs that sleep snoring"). Among the theories about the origins of the English name is one stating that it comes from the Latin *pugnus* ("fist") and another claiming that it derives from a fighting dog called Pugnaces. Alternatively, these dogs may have been named after a type of pet monkey in China.

The pug has very narrow nostrils, which radiate heat inefficiently, so these dogs have low tolerance for heat. Also, because puppies' heads are large and adults have small hips, giving birth tends to be difficult, and birth is by cesarean section about half the time. Mother dogs also have difficulty in biting off the umbilical cord because of the undershot jaw, and, for the same reason, puppies have difficulty drinking milk.

Although pugs are heavy and their legs are not strong, they are powerful and can jump somewhat, and they enjoy exercise. One owner says, "Unable to wait for their turn to walk, they moan and complain. When it rains and we cannot go for a walk, they have temper tantrums and crumple papers."

These dogs are big eaters and tend to gain weight, so their food intake should be monitored, and,

because they are indiscriminate about what they eat, their surroundings should be kept clear of small objects.

Despite their short coat, pugs shed heavily, and daily brushing is necessary. In addition, their large eyes tear easily, and frequent cleaning around the eyes is required.

Size: [male] Height: 10–11 inches; weight: 13–18 pounds
[female] same

Coat: Short and dense. Colors include apricot, black, and fawn, with black trace from back of head to tail.

Remarks: For kennel clubs, high-set double-curled tail is desirable.

Also called: *Mops Hund* (German, "pug dog"), *carlin* (French, "pug"), *carlino* (Italian, "pug"), *doguillo* (Spain, "little dog"), Dutch pug

AKC/Toy; KC/Toy

Shih Tzu

Place of origin: China

56 days

56 days

Shih tzu puppies, with their fluffy coats, look like stuffed animals that move. After scurrying around busily, they resemble snoring stuffed animals.

These dogs, treasured in the Chinese court, were regarded as holy messengers, and it is said that eunuchs in the Forbidden City strove to create types that the emperors would appreciate. Although Shih tzus were especially cherished by Ming dynasty rulers, many were killed during the Opium War.

In about 1930, some of these dogs were taken to Europe, where they were originally categorized as Lhasa apsos (which, with Pekingese, they are said to be descended from),

45 days

38 days

Size: [male] Height: less than 11 inches; weight: less than 18 pounds (9–16 pounds is ideal)
[female] same

Coat: Long and dense; undercoat is soft. All colors are permissible.

Remarks: Curled tail is carried over back.

Also called: *Shih tzu kou* (Chinese, "lion dog"); chrysanthemum dog (from facial resemblance to the flowers)

AKC/Toy; KC/Toy

but, later, the shih tzu was recognized as an independent breed.

Though these dogs are somewhat stubborn, they are usually very quiet and easygoing. As one owner says, "They often lie relaxed in their favorite place." They can exercise indoors, but they need occasional outside play. Because puppies' heads are big in comparison with adult bodies, labor can be difficult.

Frequent brushing is necessary to keep their coats beautiful, and hairpins and rubber bands can keep hair out of their faces. It is also important to keep their ears clean.

Yorkshire Terrier

Place of origin: United Kingdom

50 days

38 days

50 days

At birth, Yorkshire terrier puppies are as black as coal, with tan markings on their eyebrows, chin, ear tips, chest, and toes, but their colors lighten (and their coat lengthens) as they grow; their final coat pattern is unpredictable until 3 months. Professional breeders shave the hair of Yorkie puppies' ears to help them prick up so their dark skin can be seen. Also, their physical growth is rather slow—it takes them about 2 years to fully mature.

Because of their long, shiny coats and big, dark eyes, dogs of this breed are referred to as "jewels that move." However, although they may look like princesses, they have a Cinderella-like past. Around the mid-19th century, this breed was created by miners and mill workers to exterminate rats in their namesake region. Yorkies quickly surprised people with their beauty, though, and they were soon valued simply as pets.

These intelligent dogs are able to do whatever they are taught, but they are willful and may refuse to perform a command. Perhaps because of their terrier blood, they also feel compelled to dig holes in the yard, though they don't require much exercise. Also, despite their size, these dogs are assertive and wary, which makes them good guard dogs. It is important to train them not to bark unnecessarily, however.

Keeping their steel-gray coats shiny and beautiful requires some effort. Their long, silky hair tends to get tangled and form hairballs, making daily brushing necessary. Also, regular professional grooming is ideal.

Size: [male] Height: 6–7 inches; weight: 3–7 pounds
[female] same

Coat: Long, silky, and glossy. Colors are steel blue on body, tan on chest, and light tan on legs; feathering on head is golden tan. Ears, roots of ears, and masks are darker.

Remarks: Kennel clubs require medium-length docked tail.

AKC/Toy; KC/Toy

38 days

50 days

Akita

Place of origin: Japan

55 days

The rather small ears of Akita puppies stand up late; after a repetitive process of pricking up and folding back, they finally stand erect at 3–4 months.

The Akita, designated as a natural treasure in Japan in 1931, is descended from a midsize hound dog bred with other indigenous dogs and fighter dogs in their native northeast Japan. Once called Odate, after a location in the Akita region, they often shared the dog-fighting ring with the Tosa, another fighter breed.

Efforts to strengthen the breed continued, and they were bred with Western dogs such as mastiffs, which resulted in a declining number of true Akitas. However, a preservation movement arose during the early 20th century that began to breed out the Western lineages in an effort to return the breed to its original appearance.

This large, dignified dog has pricked ears and a curly tail—and a face thought to be reminiscent of classic Japanese aristocrats. One owner says, "No matter what happens, they don't react right away, and they check out the situation,

Size: [male] Height: about 26–28 inches; weight: about 107 pounds
[female] Height: about 23–26 inches; weight: about 89 pounds

Coat: Outer coat is hard; undercoat is soft and dense. Coat color comes in red, brindle, peppering, and white; all colors except white must have white markings on underside.

AKC/Working; KC/Utility

55 days

55 days

remaining calm." Despite its sedate demeanor, however, the Akita requires frequent exercise.

Dogs of this breed are typically obedient and loyal, but only to their owners. They are friendly enough around strangers, but only if the owner is near, and they are very strong willed, so it is important to build a trusting relationship. One owner says, "When he fails in something, he tends to get very depressed. It requires considerable effort to help him regain confidence."

The Akita's thick double coat requires daily brushing.

55 days

Alaskan Malamute

Place of origin: United States

50 days

Dogs of this breed were used by the Malemute tribe of Alaska to pull sleds and hunt, and the dogs became popular in more temperate climates after Arctic explorers employed them as sled dogs. Though Siberian huskies, which they resemble, can match them for speed, Alaskan malamutes are the world's largest and strongest sled dogs.

Because of their furry, thickly padded soles, these dogs are referred to as "sled dogs in snowshoes." Well equipped against extreme cold, they can sleep in snow and ice, even when the temperature is well below freezing, and they wrap their thick, curly tails around to muzzles to protect their faces during snowstorms.

Bred to work in teams, malamutes are obedient and friendly with people and other dogs. As one owner says, "They are big and fierce looking, but they have a childlike character.

They also boast a bottomless vitality." Another owner comments, "After bicycling alongside a running dog for one or two hours, you'll notice they are still as full of energy as before you started." However, note that, because of their thick coats, they are sensitive to heat.

Daily brushing is required to keep the coat beautiful. During the shedding season, they lose a lot of hair and require additional grooming.

Size: [male] Height: about 26 inches; weight: about 87 pounds
[female] Height: about 23 inches; weight: about 76 pounds

Coat: Rough and thick; undercoat is woolly and water repellent. Colors are a mixture of black, gray, wolf, white, and others; lower side of abdomen, mask and legs are white. Only white is accepted as a solid color.

Remarks: KC standards are larger: 26–28 inches and 23–26 inches for males and females respectively and 84–147 pounds for both.

Also called: Arctic malamute

AKC/Working; KC/Working

50 days

Bernese Mountain Dog

Place of origin: Switzerland

The Bernese mountain dog is one of various breeds of working dogs developed in each mountainous region of Switzerland. This breed, originating near Bern, was said to have been developed by crossbreeding local dogs with a type brought to the area by a Roman legion. Long used as cattle dogs, working dogs, and guard dogs, they are now popular as household pets as well.

Although these dogs look imposing and are somewhat wary, they are good natured and loyal. As one owner says, "They follow me wherever I go." They don't require much exercise, but they enjoy walking or following their owners while they jog or cycle. Their good memories make them ideal rescue dogs.

Normal brushing and occasional shampooing is sufficient; they shed little. However, their pendant ears require regular cleaning.

60 days

60 days

Size: [male] Height: 26–30 inches; weight: 80–107 pounds
[female] Height: 23–26 inches; weight: 76–91 pounds

Coat: Rich and smooth. Base color is glossy black, with tan markings on eyebrows, cheeks, and legs; chest and digits are white, and face has white blaze.

Remarks: Kennel clubs require docked tail.

Also called: *Berner Sennenhund* (German, "Bernese herding dog")

AKC/Working; KC/Working

60 days

60 days

Boxer

Place of origin: Germany

30 days

30 days

This breed was developed as a fighting dog by crossbreeding the *Bullenbeisser*, which was used to hunt deer, wild boar, and bear in Germany in the 19th century, with the bulldog. The name supposedly comes from their unique fighting style, in which they lift up their paws.

Dogs of this highly trainable breed have worked as hound dogs, working dogs, army dogs, cattle dogs, guard dogs, Seeing Eye dogs, and watchdogs, and some were selected to become the first police dogs in Germany.

With their trim, boxy bodies, chic coat colors and rather odd features, boxers are simultaneously handsome and comical looking. This distinctive look, combined with their expressiveness and good nature, makes them popular as household pets.

These independent, quick-learning dogs are basically peaceful and loyal to their owners. Nonetheless, owners should recognize that this breed is not only intelligent but also physically strong. It needs frequent exercise and lots of room to run.

Occasional light brushing is sufficient, but their nails must be clipped regularly. Also, they are very sensitive to both hot and cold weather.

30 days

Size: [male] Height: 23–26 inches; weight: about 71 pounds
[female] Height: 21–24 inches; weight: about 60 pounds

Coat: Short and glossy. Colors are variations of fawn; if brindled, stripes must be clear. White markings are permissible, and mask is black.

Remarks: Kennel clubs require docked tails and (except for KC) cropped ears.

AKC/Working; KC/Working

30 days

Bullmastiff

Place of origin: United Kingdom

51 days

51 days

Bred in England in the second half of the 19th century from the Old English mastiff and the bulldog, these large, powerful dogs—speedier and more aggressive than the former but not as savage as the latter—were called "gamekeeper's night dogs." Their job was to find and chase poachers and hold them down until the gamekeeper caught up.

These natural watchdogs look like canine tanks, but they are gentle and obedient. Because of their size and strength, however, strict obedience training is required to keep them under control. Also, they can be wary and aggressive, requiring experience and skill to handle them. They should be exposed frequently to people and other dogs.

Plenty of exercise is necessary, but, despite their short coat, they are sensitive to heat because of their size.

Size: [male] Height: 26–28 inches; weight: 111–133 pounds
[female] Height: 24–26 inches; weight: 100–120 pounds

Coat: Rough; undercoat is short and dense. Colors include silver, apricot, fawn, dark fawn, and brindle; muzzle, nose, ears, and area around eyes should be dark (the darker, the better).

AKC/Working; KC/Working

51 days

51 days

Their short coat is very easy to care for; an occasional massage with a cloth or a soft brush is sufficient. Nails should be clipped regularly, and their pendant ears require regular cleaning.

Doberman Pinscher

Place of origin: Germany

Toward the end of the 19th century, when dog shows were first held and breed improvement was popular, a German magistrate named Ludwig Dobermann, who also worked as a night guard and dog warden, developed this breed as a guard dog, using the German pinscher as the base stock and crossbreeding with the rottweiler, the Great Dane, the German shorthaired pointer, the weimaraner, the Manchester terrier, the dachshund, and other breeds.

These dogs became popular after they were widely used as army dogs in World War I. Today, in addition to still being employed by the military, they serve as guard dogs, watchdogs, and police dogs but are also popular as household pets.

Because of the Doberman's fierce look and fearsome reputation, its presence alone has tremendous impact and is often enough to scare intruders away. One owner describes the breed's charm by saying, "They are bold and delicate at the same time. They are insightful, docile and one track minded."

Although they are both very wary and courageous, they are also obedient to their owners. This is a fitting breed for both companionship and protection. However, obedience training needs to be given while they are puppies, they should be socialized around humans and other dogs, and owners of these dogs should have enough physical strength and skill to control them. They require much exercise.

The Doberman's short coat is very easy to care for; massage it with a cloth or a soft brush.

Size: [male] Height: 26–28 inches; weight: 71–76 pounds
[female] Height: 24–26 inches; weight: 60–64 pounds

Coat: Short and straight. Colors include black, brown, blue, and isabella (fawn), with rust-tan markings.

Remarks: Kennel clubs require tail docked and (except for KC) ears cropped. (Dock tail within 1 week of birth; ears should be cropped in 2–4 months.)

Also called: *Thuringer Pinscher* (German, "terrier from Thuringia," a German state), *Plizelich Soldatenhund* (German, "Plizelich soldier dog"); Dobermann (KC)

AKC/Working; KC/Working

43 days

75 days

43 days

Dogo Argentino

Place of origin: Argentina

35 days

At birth, dogo Argentino puppies are white, but patterns emerge in their coats as they mature. Precociously independent and willful from a young age, these puppies must undergo rigorous training. Also, though rough play with their siblings is natural, they like to gnaw on things.

This very rare dog looks, from a distance, something like a white Labrador retriever. The breed, whose name is Spanish for "Argentine bulldog," was created by two young brothers named Antonio Nores and Augustin Martinez by crossbreeding their earlier creation, the Cordoba fighting dog, with a variety of breeds to incorporate many qualities into one dog, including pointers (sharp sense of smell), Irish wolfhounds (sense), bull terriers (courage), Spanish mastiffs (strength), Great Danes (mass), and Great Pyrenees (coat). They were used to hunt aggressive big game such as pumas, jaguars, and wild boars. One owner says of the dogs of this breed, "Dressed in a white satin coat, they have hearts of gold in bodies of steel."

Prospective owners should have the strength, determination, and skill to keep this powerful dogs under control. Also, although they can endure great heat, they are sensitive to cold.

35 days

Size: [male] Height: 24–28 inches;
weight: 80–100 pounds
[female] same

Coat: Short and smooth. Color is white.

Remarks: Skin color should be pink; dark
skin not acceptable.

Also called: Argentinian mastiff,
Argentine dog

AKC/Unrecognized; KC/Unrecognized

35 days

Giant Schnauzer

Place of origin: Germany

This breed, a jumbo-size version of the standard schnauzer whose height is about twice that of the miniature schnauzer, was bred to herd cows and other large farm animals. In its place of origin, this breed was once referred to as the *Münchener* (German, "from Munich").

To increase this breed's size, it was crossbred with such large dogs as the Great Dane, the rottweiler, the Bouvier des Flandres, and the local sheepdog. These intelligent, highly trainable, keen-smelling dogs worked as police dogs in Japan before World War II.

Although there is nothing flashy about these simple, sturdy dogs, their form is beautiful and they are very amicable.

Aside from size, the standards for this breed are almost the same as those for the standard schnauzer. The coat colors are also the same, but black and tan are also accepted for the giant schnauzer.

Daily brushing and combing and regular trimming are necessary, and dead hair and hair with split ends must be stripped.

30 days

30 days

30 days

Size: [male] Height: 26–28 inches; weight: 76–96 pounds
[female] Height: 24–26 inches; weight: 67–89 pounds

Coat: Hard and wiry; hair on back stands up slightly. Colors include salt-and-pepper, black, and black and tan; white chest markings permissible.

Remarks: Kennel clubs require docked tail and (except for KC) cropped ears.

Also called: *Riesenschnauzer* (German, "large schnauzer")

AKC/Working; KC/Working

30 days

30 days

30 days

Great Dane

Place of origin: Germany

Great Dane puppies undergo a rapid and drastic transformation from kitten-size newborns to calf-size dogs, but their bones and muscles are slow to mature, so take care not to exercise them excessively when they are young.

This breed was developed by crossbreeding the boarhound—named for its aggressive quarry—with the Tibetan mastiff, the Old English mastiff, and the greyhound, retaining the dignity of the first two breeds and the elegance of the latter one, but the details of its origins are unknown. The breed name derives from the United Kingdom, where one of several French names for it, *grand danois* ("big Danish"), was slightly modified in the translation.

This expressive breed, called the "Apollo of dogs," appears to be unapproachably imposing, but one owner says, "They are a little stubborn, fairly delicate, and shy. They love to be babied." Nonetheless, they are friendly only to their owners.

Although these quick-learning dogs are gentle giants, they are powerful, and owners of this breed should train them well from puppyhood. Also, note that they require not only a great deal of time (and space) for exercise but also a prodigious amount of food.

As their coat is short, it is easy to care for; an occasional brushing is sufficient.

46 days

46 days

46 days

Size: [male] Height: 31–32 inches;
weight: 120–144 pounds
[female] Height: 28–30 inches;
weight: 100–122 pounds

Coat: Short and glossy. Colors include
brindle, fawn, blue, black, and harlequin
(black patches).

Remarks: Kennel clubs (except KC and
those in Germany) require cropped ears.

Also called: *Deutsche Dogge* (German,
"German dog")

AKC/Working; KC/Working

Great Pyrenees

Places of origin: France and Spain

Fluffy Great Pyrenees puppies, resembling rolling snowballs (it is said "they have brought life to the snowdrifts of the Pyrenees"), are cheerful and active but very cautious. At birth, they weigh 21–29 ounces; by 1 month, their weight increases tenfold, and by 6 months it is 5 times larger than that.

Images of dogs closely resembling this breed are found in the ruins of the European Bronze Age (17th–10th centuries B.C.) and among Babylonian works of art. It is hard to

31 days

imagine that these tranquil, tender-looking dogs, with their beautiful white coats, have such a venerable, vigorous history, but, armed with spiked iron collars, they long reigned as invincible protectors of sheep, warding off not only wolves, bears and wild dogs but also rustlers in the Pyrenees Mountains, on the Spanish-French border.

There have been many heroic stories about Great Pyrenees throughout the centuries, but it was not until the reign of Louis XVII in the late 18th century that this breed won special favor with the French royal family.

They are willful dogs, though. As one owner says, "When he is not satisfied, he will come to me to complain. He doesn't care that I'm his owner. He is like a man in a Great Pyrenees' coat."

Brushing every few days is sufficient, except when extra effort is required during the shedding season; their hair doesn't tangle.

31 days

Size: [male] Height: 31–32 inches; weight: 111–133 pounds [female] Height: 26–30 inches; weight: 100–122 pounds

Coat: Thick, slightly wavy. Colors on undercoat are white, dark brown on white, and gray and tan on white.

Also called: *Chien de montagne des pirénées* (French, "dog of the Pyrenees Mountains"); Pyrenean mountain dog (KC)

AKC/Working; KC/Pastoral

31 days

Leonberger

Place of origin: Germany

Size: [male] Height: 30–32 inches;
weight: about 89 pounds
[female] same

Coat: Long and flat; undercoat is dense.
Rich feathering on tail. Colors include lion
gold, red, reddish brown, sand (fawn,
cream), and combinations of these colors;
mask is black.

AKC/Unrecognized; KC/Working

31 days

31 days

31 days

31 days

31 days

31 days

These fluffy Newfoundland-like puppies start out very small but grow swiftly.

Nineteenth-century Leonberg, Germany, town councillor Heinrich Essig, a devoted dog breeder, wished to develop a breed resembling the lion depicted in the town emblem. Ultimately, the breed was created by mating a Newfoundland and a Saint Bernard kept in the namesake monastery, and then a dog from that litter was bred to a Great Pyrenees.

These leonine dogs were sold to world leaders such as Napoleon III and Otto von Bismarck, and eventually they spread out, albeit thinly, all over the world. After World War I, however, only five Leonbergers were alive, but they were treasured, and efforts were made to multiply the breed. World War II dealt another blow to the still-modest number of these dogs, however, and only 8 survived. It took another 25 years to revive the breed.

These tranquil, obedient dogs seldom bark, love to be around people, and are good with children. Nonetheless, they can become too powerful to control, so good training is essential. They need lots of exercise.

Their gorgeous, water-repellent coat (they have webbed toes and are excellent swimmers) requires daily brushing, especially during the shedding season, when dead hair should be carefully removed.

Newfoundland

Place of origin: Canada

68 days

68 days

Newborn Newfoundland puppies, docile and teddy-bearish, weigh as much as 21–29 ounces, and their weight exceeds 22 pounds by about 2 months. Later, however, they grow slowly, taking about 2 years to fully mature.

Although the origin and lineage of these dogs is uncertain, they long helped fishermen and pulled freight carts on the namesake Canadian island, and they are also renowned as rescue dogs for disasters at sea.

These excellent swimmers, bred to work in and around cold ocean waters, are unfazed by cold water or weather. They have a waterproof double coat and especially large paws and feet for producing strong strokes, and the thick skin between their toes functions as a web.

Just like literature's best-known Newfoundland, Nana, from J. M. Barrie's *Peter Pan*, these dogs make good playmates for children, but when they frolic too much, they can

be a handful. Another artistic contribution to their popularity is a portrait of a Newfoundland with a black-and-white coat by 19th-century artist Sir Henry Edwin Landseer; this coat, named after the painter, has since then became popular.

These fast, powerful dogs are nevertheless sensitive to heat and prone to drool and snore.

Newfoundlands shed a lot, and their thick coat must be brushed often. After water play, it should be dried.

Size: [male] Height: about 28 inches; weight: 131–151 pounds
[female] Height: about 26 inches; weight: 100–120 pounds

Coat: Flat, dense. Colors include black, brown, and Landseer (black and white); FCI recognizes Landseer as a separate breed.

Remarks: Tail hangs long and end curves upward.

AKC/Working; KC/Pastoral

(Landseer)

60 days

Rottweiler

Place of origin: Germany

45 days

45 days

Large-boned rottweiler puppies look like adult dogs that have been down-sized and wadded up. Also, contrary to their innocent looks, these puppies can be a handful.

The rottweiler's ancestors are dogs that herded cows to feed Roman soldiers and supported the legions in their expeditions through Europe. The breed was later developed to handle heavy physical labor by butchers and cattle merchants in Rottweil, Germany, which was then thriving as a border market town.

As donkeys took over their cargo-handling work, these dogs lost their

45 days

45 days

Size: [male] Height: 24–28 inches; weight: about 116 pounds [female] Height: 22–26 inches; weight: about 100 pounds

Coat: Hard, dense, short. Colors are black and tan, with tan markings above eyes and on muzzle and cheeks, as well as on chest and at fixed places on legs.

Remarks: Kennel clubs require docked tail.

AKC/Working; KC/Working

value and became almost extinct. However, their talent and undaunted courage were recognized, and they made a comeback as police dogs. Even now, they are tough and tenacious hard workers that can survive on a frugal diet, but they have become popular as household pets.

Reliable, hardworking rottweilers nevertheless require training to enhance their natural qualities. They have strong self-protective instincts and are wary around other dogs, so they must be socialized. Females tend to be more obedient and less independent and therefore easier to handle.

Owners must be physically strong to control the large, powerful males, and it is best to have only one dog in a household. Also, they need daily vigorous exercise.

Saint Bernard

Place of origin: Switzerland

The Saint Bernard, the national dog of Switzerland and the companion dog of old Alm-Uncle in Johanna Spyri's classic children's novel, *Heidi,* is said to be descended partially from the Tibetan mastiff.

For about 300 years, these dogs, at the time smaller and leaner and with shorter hair, lived in the monastery of Saint Bernard on the Italian-Swiss border. Trained as rescue dogs, they used their acute sense of smell to find people lost in the mountains and their strength to pull these weak or injured travelers on sleds in the snow; during this period, they were credited with saving more than 2,000 people.

This breed, although it takes a backseat to the Irish wolfhound as far as height is concerned (despite one specimen that stood 53 inches), is the heaviest in the world. Their large paws and feet are equipped with strong toes that bend upward to help keep them from slipping on snow and ice. Bred for alpine conditions (they are said to be able to sense approaching avalanches and storms), they are sensitive to heat.

55 days

31 days

Saint Bernards must be trained carefully from puppyhood so that they can be controlled easily despite their size. As one breeder says, "From the first day you take them out for a walk, it is important not to let them walk ahead of you."

Frequent brushing is required, as well as cleaning of their pendant ears, and their muzzles need to be wiped occasionally.

Size: [male] Height: at least 28 inches; weight: about 167 pounds
[female] Height: at least 26 inches; weight: about 147 pounds

Coat: Long and short varieties. Colors include red with white, white with red, variations of red, and brindle; white markings on mask, blaze, collar, chest, and legs.

Remarks: Long tail is carried low. KC standards do not specify a height but do state that the taller, the better, as long as it has a well-balanced build.

Also called: *Saint Bernardshund* (German, "Saint Bernard's dog"); *Bernhardiner* (German, "of Bernard"); Saint Bernard dog

AKC/Working; KC/Working

55 days

Samoyed

Place of origin: Russia

80 days

50 days

These dogs, long used by the aboriginal Samoyeds on the tundras of Siberia as watchdogs and sled dogs, were employed on the Scott and Amundsen Antarctic expeditions.

Dogs of this breed (first registered as the Samoyede, though the name was later revised to Samoyed), are considered to be gifts from the angels, and the upturned corners of their mouths give these friendly dogs, nicknamed Sammy or Sam, an infectiously happy look.

One owner says, "They try to be babied and loved even by someone they've just met for the first time. They may follow anyone." Another owner comments, "These dogs don't care about little things. They are really carefree."

Sable or black-and-white coats, which look especially beautiful against a snowy background, were popular once, but once they were introduced to England, their coat colors were restricted to pure white, biscuit, and cream.

The hairy, padded toes of these snow-loving dogs spread so they can grip snowy ground, and they protect their muzzles with their bushy tails to protect them from the cold air when they sleep. They also like to play in water year-round, but they are sensitive to heat.

Frequent brushing and combing are necessary, especially during the shedding seasons.

Size: [male] Height: 21–28 inches; weight: 56–71 pounds
[female] Height: 19–21 inches; weight: 40–56 pounds

Coat: Long and straight; undercoat is soft and dense. Colors include pure white, cream, and biscuit.

Remarks: Sizes vary according to kennel clubs. Tail is long and curled over back.

Also called: *Samoiedskaja Sabaka* (Russian, "Samoyed dog")

AKC/Working; KC/Pastoral

80 days

50 days

50 days

Siberian Husky

Place of origin: Russia

40 days

40 days

40 days

Facial markings are more distinct on puppies, but, by about 4–5 months, they are reduced to eyeglass-type rims and disappear at about 1 year.

These dogs, less powerful but faster than the Alaskan malamute, were developed from the sled dogs of the Chukchi peoples of northeast Asia. Their name comes from the same word that became *Eskimo*, though it's alternatively said to derive from their throaty howling. Dense hair between their toes gives them traction, so they are able to grab snowy and icy surfaces.

Though these modestly friendly dogs are less popular than they used to be, they make good pets for active people. One owner says, "They don't become too close to you. They are rather cool and blunt, but they love people and are caring."

Because of their arctic origin, huskies are nearly impervious to cold and sensitive to heat. They require lots of exercise; because they tend to

40 days

40 days

wander, run them on a leash, and, if possible, occasionally let them pull a sled or a cart. A smaller, pointy-faced variety has appeared, but, due to careless breeding, it tends to have character problems.

Their thick, soft coat requires frequent brushing and combing, especially during the shedding period, when they lose a lot of hair.

Size: [male] Height: 21–24 inches; weight: 44–60 pounds
[female] Height: 20–22 inches; weight: 36–51 pounds

Coat: Rich and straight; undercoat is soft and fluffy. As long as white is mixed, any coat colors are accepted; distinctive markings appear on head and face.

Remarks: Foxlike tail.

Also called: Siberian Chukchi; arctic husky

AKC/Working; KC/Working

40 days

Standard Schnauzer

Place of origin: Germany

75 days

75 days

Standard schnauzer puppies become independent quite early; their trademark whiskers develop late.

This breed, the original of the three schnauzer varieties, was long used to catch rats and guard farmyards in its place of origin, but no information about it predates the 14th century. Standard schnauzers also have a good reputation as waterfowl hounds, and their talent as sheepdogs is highly valued.

These dogs are intelligent, excellent in judgment, and highly trainable, enjoying both physical and mental exercise, although one breeder says, "This breed seems to display their good nature better when they are raised indoors rather than outdoors." One owner comments, "As they grow older, they become wiser. They seem to accumulate knowledge." They're undaunted by heights and have excellent spring to their leaps.

Daily combing, especially of the feathering on the legs and abdomen, and quarterly trimming are required, and stripping is important.

75 days

75 days

Size: [male] Height: 18–20 inches; weight: 27–40 pounds
[female] Height: 17–19 inches; weight: 22–33 pounds

Coat: Short and wiry; colors include salt-and-pepper, and black.

Remarks: Kennel clubs require docked tail and (except KC) cropped ears.

Also called: Schnauzer (KC)

AKC/Working; KC/Working

Bichon Frise

Place of origin: France

43 days

43 days

Newborn puppies are all white, with pink noses and short coats, but their noses gradually turn black and their coats grow long and fluffy after up to 2 years. After 8 months, the coat develops a double layer, which tends to form hair balls.

These dogs are said to have been discovered by 14th-century Italian sailors on Tenerife in the Canary Islands, off the northwest coast of Africa, from which they were brought back to Europe. In France in the 1500s, these chic-looking, powder-puffy dogs were downsized and became popular accessories among French and Italian noblewomen, who perfumed them and decorated them with ribbons, calling them "white lappers." (Their name is a shortened translation, from French, of "curly-haired lapdog.")

Other dogs in the Mediterranean-based *bichon* (French, "lapdog") group, which is closely related to the poodle, are the Maltese and the less well-known Bolonais and Havanais, all of which are said be partly descended from the barbet and the water spaniel.

Size: [male] Height: 10–12 inches; weight: 7–11 pounds
[female] same

Coat: Long, curly, and silky; undercoat is soft. Colors include white, cream, and apricot; slight gray on ears and body is permissible.

Remarks: Tail is carried over back.

Also called: *Bichon à poil frisé* (French, "curly-haired lapdog")

AKC/Non-Sporting; KC/Toy

43 days

Perhaps because of their lapdog legacy, dogs of this cheerful breed interact well with people. One owner says, "They have a natural genius for-fawning." They are ideal indoor dogs, as they don't bark unnecessarily, have almost no canine odor, and lose little hair.

The bichon frise became popular worldwide after a unique coat-trimming style, created a few decades ago in the United States, was adopted, giving it the appearance of carrying cotton candy on its head.

Frequent care is required to maintain the bichon frise's elegant coat.

43 days

Boston Terrier

Place of origin: United States

Newborn Boston terrier puppies are born with their ears flat against their heads. Sooner or later, depending on the ears' size and thickness, they will prick halfway up, then warp backward, bend forward, and finally stand up straight. Typical of dogs with undershot mouths, these puppies have difficulty nursing and, initially, eating solid food, and they tend to snore until they are older.

Although most terriers originated in the United Kingdom, this breed was bred in its namesake city in the United States during the second half of the 19th century by crossbreeding the English bulldog with the white English terrier. Larger at first, they were reduced in size by being crossbred with the French bulldog. Because this dog's coat suggests a tuxedo-wearing canine, the breed is sometimes referred to as the "American gentleman dog."

Boston terriers are especially mischievous, but they are affectionate, and one owner says, "They are good at winning the hearts and minds of people." A brief daily session of exercise is necessary.

Their short, glossy coat requires only occasional wiping with a rough cloth.

28 days

37 days

37 days

37 days

Size: [male] Height: 10–16 inches; weight: 11–24 pounds [female] same

Coat: Short and silky. Color is ideally brindle, with white markings, but black with white markings is permissible.

Remarks: Short tail has straight, crank, and screw variations. Kennel clubs (except KC) require cropped ears.

AKC/Non-Sporting; KC/Utility

37 days

28 days

Bulldog

Place of origin: United Kingdom

Non-Sporting Group

From 1150 to 1815, when dogfighting was banned in England, these dogs were employed in bullbaiting, hence their name. Bred for their suitability for this cruel sport of attacking tethered bulls and giving them a final mortal bite on the nose, dogs of this breed have a squashed face that enabled them to breathe while biting the bull and a compact, muscular body to complement their combative spirit and ferocity. The legacy of this genetic engineering also includes snoring and drooling, and, because newborn bulldog puppies' heads are so large, they are usually delivered by cesarean section.

The bulldog, however, has since become a cheerful, friendly, expressive, peaceful and obedient dog and is very popular as an intelligent and winsome household pet.

Because of their short muzzles, they cannot control their body temperature well and are sensitive to heat. Also, their food intake should be monitored.

Coat care is simple, but keeping these dogs clean requires a little effort: Wipe between their wrinkles, and regularly clean their eyes, ears, and muzzles.

88 days

50 days

88 days

88 days

Size: [male] Height: 12–16 inches; weight: about 56 pounds
[female] Height: 12–16 inches; weight: about 51 pounds

Coat: Short and dense. Colors include red brindle and other brindles, as well as solid colors such as white, red, fawn, and fallow, and white-and-red and white-and-black mixtures.

Remarks: Short tail has straight, crank, and screw variations.

Also called: English bulldog

AKC/Non-Sporting; KC/Utility

88 days

Chow Chow

Place of origin: China

39 days

39 days

Chow chow puppies, resembling bear cubs, require little effort. One owner says, "They are quiet and not mischievous. They don't insist on being played with. Adult dogs are the same. They are really fuss free."

This breed's history is reputed to go back 3,000 years, but concrete information is available only from about 150 B.C. Theories about its origin tend to emphasize the breed's use as a food source, but they also were known to work as hound dogs, sled dogs, and guard dogs. Several theories persist about the origin of their breed name.

The saintly, unperturbed nature of dogs of this breed is matched by their loyalty to their owners, although they are never given to fawning. One owner says, "Even if other dogs try to pick a fight, these dogs ignore them." However, they are fearless and highly protective, although they rarely bark.

39 days

When mature, they gain quite a bit of weight and grow featherings around their neck like a lion's mane. Black chow chows look like hairy bears, and, with their blue-black tongues, their appearance is striking.

Their straight, stiltlike hind legs make them slow, rather clumsy runners, supposedly a legacy of their use as stock. They do enjoy exercise, however, although they are sensitive to heat.

Brushing every other day is sufficient, except during the shedding season. Also, dogs with deep-set eyes may have trouble with ingrown eyelashes.

Size: [male] Height: 19–22 inches; weight: 49–67 pounds
[female] Height: 18–20 inches; weight: 36–56 pounds

Coat: Rough and dense; undercoat is woolly. Colors include red, cream, fawn, black, and blue.

Remarks: Tail is carried on back.

AKC/Non-Sporting; KC/Utility

Dalmatian

Place of origin: Croatia

41 days

41 days

Newborn dalmatian puppies are snow white; the trademark spots of this breed appear, little by little, within 10–14 days. The color, shape, size, and number of the spots are unpredictable.

These dogs were first found in the Balkan province from which they take their name, but records and stories about dogs that resemble this breed are found in many places in Europe and western Asia. They were said to have an uncanny ability to calm horses, and they used to be called coach dogs and carriage dogs, from the era in which they escorted horse-drawn vehicles (including fire wagons and, more recently, fire trucks, leading to their traditional role as firehouse mascots), and were also, based on their appearance, nicknamed spotted dogs and plum-pudding dogs.

Dalmations have also worked as guard dogs, circus dogs, military dogs, farmyard watchdogs, and bird hounds, scent hounds, and hound dogs, as well as in other roles. Later, these dogs increasingly became household pets after they were popularized by the classic children's novel

Size: [male] Height: 23–24 inches; Weight: 49–64 pounds [female] Height: 22–23 inches; Weight: 49–55 pounds

Coat: Short, hard, and dense. Color is pure white, with black or liver spots. Kennel clubs prefer small, round, dark, and plentiful spots.

Remarks: Tail hangs down; curled tail is not permissible.

AKC/Non-Sporting; KC/Utility

41 days

41 days

101 Dalmatians and its animated and live film adaptations.

Dogs of this peaceful, intelligent breed are friendly to their owners but aloof toward other people. They make good watchdogs, but they need long exercise sessions.

Their coats are very easy to care for, but watch for allergic dermatitis, or inflammation of the skin.

41 days

French Bulldog

Place of origin: France

43 days

43 days

50 days

50 days

The French bulldog's trademark large, batlike ears lie flat on newborn puppies, but they cycle through standing and drooping several times before they finally prick up for good.

Excessive exercise should be avoided until puppies are grown.

Although the English bulldog is widely believed to be this breed's ancestor, opinion is divided as to whether the French bulldog was bred from small toy-type dogs of the former breed brought by British immigrants to northern France during the second half of the 19th century or whether French bulldogs are an older breed that were already being used for dogfighting in the 1600s. Besides their ears, which were once allowed to prick up or be half bent, their domed head is the breed's distinguishing feature.

These dogs are well loved for their misleadingly imposing appearance; they are actually gentle, quiet, intelligent dogs that don't bark unnecessarily. However, because of their short muzzles, they are known to snore. This characteristic also makes them sensitive to heat, and, because

Size: [male] Height: about 12 inches; Weight: 18–22 pounds
[female] same

Coat: Short and glossy. Colors include dark brindle, brindle and white, and fawn.

Remarks: Short tail is either straight or screw variation.

Also called: *Bouledogue français* (French, "French bulldog")

AKC/Non-Sporting; KC/Utility

50 days

of their unusually large heads, litters are delivered by cesarean section.

Their short coats generally need little care, except during the shedding season, when frequent brushing is needed; also, check for skin conditions. In addition, the ears, eyes, nose, and muzzle need to be cleaned, and their nails should be clipped regularly.

43 days

Lhasa Apso

Place of origin: Tibet

71 days

71 days

This 2,000-year-old breed's homeland is the foothills of the Himalayas. Believed to ward off evil spirits and bring good luck, these dogs were kept by priests and noblemen in Lhasa, home of Lama monasteries. The breed name is said to derive from the Tibetan phrase *Lhasa apso seng kye*, which means "a leonine dog from Lhasa that barks well." Another interpretation translates the phrase to "a leonine dog from Lhasa that is as hairy as a goat" (*apso* means "goat").

Although these dogs were for many years not allowed out of the region, the Dalai Lamas used to make an exception and offer male dogs to the Chinese emperors. They were not kept to entertain local or far-flung noblemen, however. From way back, these intelligent, wary, and sharp-of-hearing dogs guarded monasteries and palaces.

One owner says, "When my dog was a puppy, he was very quiet, and only on rare occasions did he bleat in a faint voice, but once he was grown up, he changed. As soon as he senses something suspicious, he barks loud and continuously." And, although Lhasa apsos are cheerful and love to play with people, they are also proud. One owner says, "They don't like to be ordered around." They are active dogs, but extensive exercise is not necessary.

Careful daily brushing is indispensable to maintain a shiny, tangle-free coat, and they should be groomed more extensively once or twice a week.

71 days

71 days

Size: [male] Height: 10–11 inches; weight: about 16 pounds
[female] Height: 9–10 inches; weight: about 13 pounds

Coat: Long, straight, and hard; undercoat is moderate and dense. Colors include gold, sand, black, honey, grizzle, and smoke.

Remarks: Feathered tail is carried over back.

Also called: Tibetan apso; *Abso Seng Kye*, the "Bark Lion Sentinel Dog"

AKC/Non-Sporting; KC/Utility

71 days

Poodle

Place of origin: Central Europe

42 days (Toy)

(Toy)

33 days (Toy)

42 days (Toy)

(Toy)

33 days (Toy)

The poodle puppy's coat color changes as it grows, and it takes about two years before it acquires its full coat.

The origin of this very old breed, which now consists of standard, miniature, and toy varieties, is not certain, but it most likely came from Germany; the name derives from *Pudel* (German, "to splash in water"). It is also known as the French poodle, a name earned because the breed later achieved fame as elegant dogs in France.

Despite their affected air, they were originally used as retrievers in watery areas; their distinctive coat-trimming pattern was designed to make it easier for them to swim and

(continued on page 198)

to protect their hearts, and the leg tufts served as makeshift fins and buoys. Recently, low-maintenance trimming that makes them look like teddy bears has increased the popularity of the two smaller varieties.

Intelligent and quick to learn, these dogs were long appreciated as stars in French dog playhouses and traveling circuses, and they continue to be circus stars. Among their more mundane tasks were pulling milk carts in Germany, and, during World War II, carrying supplies and messages. Among this breed's many fans throughout history was Beethoven, who composed music in memory of his beloved poodle.

Small poodles are excitable, but because they are generally quiet and peaceful, they are suitable for families with children.

These dogs don't shed, but their hair grows fast, requiring regular trimming and careful brushing.

Size: STANDARD [male] Height: about 15 inches or more; weight: 46–71 pounds [female] same
MINIATURE [male] Height: 11–15 inches; weight: 7–13 pounds [female] same
TOY [male] Height: about 10 inches or less; weight: 4–7 pounds [female] same

Coat: Rich, dense, and curly or corded. Colors include black, white, apricot, blue, and cream; solid colors are ideal.

Remarks: Kennel clubs require docked tail.

Also called: French poodle; *caniche* (French, "shaggy dog")

AKC/Non-Sporting (toy poodle categorized in Toy Group); KC/Utility

(Miniature)

60 days (Miniature)

(Standard)

90 days (Miniature)

(Miniature)

60 days

60 days (Miniature)

Schipperke

Place of origin: Belgium

In 19th-century Belgium, schipperkes (Flemish for "little skippers"), developed by miniaturizing black sheepdogs called Leauvenaars—considered the ancestor of the Belgian sheepdog (Groenendael) as well—served as mascots for barges traveling on the canals between Brussels and Antwerp.

76 days

76 days

76 days

Their tails were said to be docked to make it easier for them to move around on barges, although a traditional story tells how the custom derived from a man who cut his schipperke's tail off because the dog stole food.

They have curious dark eyes, mobile ears, and no tail. One owner says, "People often take these puppies for animals other than dogs."

These winsome, fawning, active dogs are wary toward strangers, so they make good watchdogs. "These dogs are very sensitive to noises," one owner comments. "I have never seen them fast asleep."

Their water-repellent coat needs only occasional brushing, although they lose a lot of hair during the shedding period and require more frequent care; also, watch for skin conditions.

Size: [male] Height: about 12 inches; weight: about 18 pounds
[female] same

Coat: Rich but somewhat hard; undercoat is soft and dense; longer, capelike hair behind neck. Black coats are standard, but (except for AKC) any solid colors are acceptable.

Remarks: Kennel clubs require docked tail; occasionally born tailless.

AKC/Non-Sporting; KC/Utility

76 days

Shar-Pei

Place of origin: China

28 days

The unique baggy wrinkles of this unusual breed (its name, in Chinese, means "hanging skin" or "sand skin") are actually more pronounced on puppies; as they grow, the wrinkles will stretch and diminish slightly.

In 1978, this obscure breed became known worldwide when it was introduced in the *Guinness Book of Records* as the world's rarest dog. Their wrinkled bodies, small ears, deep-set eyes, and black-blue tongues also make them one of the most distinctive-looking breeds, but their origins are modest. Long ago, in Guangdong, China, they were used as hound dogs, farmyard watchdogs, fighting dogs, and, sometimes, even food. Their wrinkles were developed to make it difficult for them to be injured fatally when they were bitten during dogfights, and their deep-set eyes are also a protective feature. They used to be larger, weighing about twice as much as they typically do now, and one was said to weigh 156 pounds.

These imposing, dignified, independent, and somewhat stubborn dogs are affectionate to their owners

28 days

28 days

28 days

but wary of other people and tend to dislike living with other dogs. They require lots of exercise.

Although the coat, which feels bristly or sandy, is deeply wrinkled, it is short and therefore easy to care for. Occasional massages with a brush or towel are sufficient, but the spaces between the wrinkles must be cleaned carefully.

Size: [male] Height: 18–20 inches; weight: 40–51 pounds
[female] Height: 16–18 inches; weight: 36–44 pounds

Coat: Short, straight, and hard. Colors include red, black, fawn, cream, and (AKC only) white.

Remarks: Tail is carried over back or bent to either side.

Also called: Chinese fighting dog

AKC/Non-Sporting; KC/Utility

Shiba Inu

Place of origin: Japan

50 days

Newborn shiba inu puppies have dark coats and look like raccoons or fox cubs, but, as they grow older, their color lightens; the darker the initial colors are, the more beautiful red they will turn. After about 1 month, their ears stand and their tails become firm. Also, their character settles early, so training should begin at about 3 months.

The most common native breed in Japan, the archetypal shiba inu, a hound dog developed to chase birds and small animals, is well suited for the country's climate. *Shiba* derives from either the Japanese term for brushwood, the bark of which their coat resembles in color, or an archaic word meaning "a small thing." (*Inu* means "dog.")

This breed is distinguished by its curled or sickle tail and triangular pricked ears. These active, intelligent, brave, simple, and noble dogs, designated as a natural treasure in Japan in 1937, require plenty of exercise.

Size: [male] Height: 15–17 inches; weight: about 20 pounds
[female] Height: 14–15 inches; weight: about 18 pounds

Coat: Straight and hard; undercoat is soft and dense. Coat colors come in red, black peppering, red peppering, black, and liver; white markings on lower muzzle.

Also called: Japanese shiba inu (KC)

AKC/Working; KC/Utility

42 days

42 days

42 days

50 days

Tibetan Spaniel

Place of origin: Tibet

57 days

57 days

57 days

This very old breed, kept mainly in monasteries and cherished by the Dalai Lamas, is believed to share an ancestor with the Pekingese. Tibetan spaniels traditionally watched over villages below monasteries and warned their watchdog partners, the Tibetan mastiffs, about human or animal intruders.

One owner says, "My dog knows to step back and observe the situation. When I come home, he first sits and looks at me as if to study me. He never jumps at me blindly like other dogs. Only when I tell him to come, he comes to me. He is always trying to read my lips, and never demands his way." These intelligent, cheerful, active dogs require frequent exercise but are quite at home inside and outside; they remain excellent watchdogs.

Coat care is simple; to keep hair from entangling, brush the coat two or three times a week.

Size: [male] Height: about 10 inches; weight: 9–16 pounds
[female] same

Coat: Silky; featherings on ears, legs, and tail. Colors include golden, black, white, sand, and any other solid colors, as well as combinations.

AKC/Non-Sporting; KC/Utility

116 days

31 days

Puppy Days Are for Learning Through Play, . . .

Whether frisking about, fighting, or exploring, puppies learn everything necessary for survival through their interactions with their siblings and parents.

In addition, puppies acquire communication skills through group play, and even apparent mischief serves as physical and mental exercise. Nothing in their play is without purpose.

When a puppy lowers its head, elevates its bottom, and wags its tail—or if it rubs its nose against you—it is sending the message: "Play with me!" Beyond the joy of joining a puppy in play, this activity provides good teaching opportunities.

Golden retriever
41 days

. . . Sleeping, and Dreaming

As their canid cousins are still, dogs were originally somewhat nocturnal animals, active primarily in the evening and early morning. Now that they are domesticated, their life patterns have adjusted to suit their human companions, who generally work during the day and sleep at night.

Nevertheless, dogs don't sleep as deeply nor for as long in one session as people do. While dogs sleep about the same amount as humans, they do so in cycles of waking and brief sleeping. Puppies, like children, sleep longer.

Dogs also apparently dream, during which they move their legs, mouths, and eyes, wag their tails, and bark. For puppies, the lessons and games of the day are played all over again at night.

English setter
38 days

Appendix

Bichon frise
43 days

Raising Puppies

By Reiko Goshima, dog trainer

Raising Puppies Is Like Raising Children

The opening scene of the animated Disney film *101 Dalmatians* depicts dogs of various breeds being walked by their owners—who look like nothing less than human versions of their pets. This scene always gets a chuckle because we know that it's true. Dogs and their owners are often very much alike not only in appearance but also in character. Why? Because a dog will take after the person who raises it.

Raising puppies is a lot like raising children. They need to be fed and protected, taught how to behave in the world, and most of all loved. If you trust your parental instincts and feelings, you will be successful at raising puppies. Nothing special is required; simply treat them as you would treat your children.

The only way bringing up puppies is different than raising children is that dogs are being taught to live among a different species, but otherwise the process is very similar. Every parent knows that raising children is not as simple as feeding them and watching them grow. Children must learn from and be socialized by their parents, siblings, teachers, and friends, and likewise puppies need to learn from their owners how to follow the regulations of human society. If in your training you make allowances for their behavior because they are dogs, you will end up teaching them halfheartedly or incompletely. Dogs need a great deal of consistent and patient guidance.

Just as parents must come to accept their children for who they are, and just as parents never stop caring for and loving their children even after they have grown and left the house, so you must have the same mind-set when raising a puppy. There are no concrete how-to's. Each puppy is different, with its own personality, its own strengths and weaknesses, and you should train your young dog in the manner most suitable for its character. If you remember to always balance this training with love and enthusiasm, you will be successful.

Pomeranian
54 days

One owner I assisted felt insecure about owning a dog because she believed she had failed at child rearing. "I couldn't raise my child right, and so I won't be able to raise a dog," she lamented. After we began training her dog together, however, she said, "Raising isn't that difficult! How come I didn't realize this while I was raising my child? I should have had a dog-raising experience first!"

Papillon
42 days

The Relationship Between Humans and Dogs

Humans and dogs have lived and worked with each other for thousands of years. They have always been good partners. One of the best examples today is the bond between the Inuit of Arctic North America and their dogs. They complement each other in the essential activities of life, from catching their quarry and carrying it to sharing it for food.

Throughout history, dogs have performed tasks that people cannot do or that dogs can do better, and they have assisted people in their lives. There are police dogs, service dogs, and Seeing Eye dogs, in addition to the millions of pets who offer companionship and often share in the familial bond of a household. In many ways, dogs are the animal that lives closest to humans.

Nonetheless, even though you may love your dog as as a member of your family, you should not treat it the same way you would treat a human. Dogs have particular needs that must be respected and attended to, and in return dogs must learn to respect the rules of the household in which they live.

In every house, there are unique rules and expectations of each person, and these vary according to each person's status. The rules for your dog should be simple and clear, and deviations should not be allowed. By nature, a dog will take charge of its "pack" if no one else exercises ultimate authority, and unclear or weakly enforced rules only teach a dog that no one is in charge.

For example, if a child takes candy without permission or plays loud music late at night, an allowance might be made for one reason or another. Circumstances and explanations can be discussed, as can expectations and consequences for the future. But a dog cannot be reasoned with in the same way. If a dog grabs food from the kitchen counter or barks late at night, it will continue these behaviors until they are consistently and firmly stopped. A dog is a living partner in your household, but it is not human. It must abide by its own set of rules and standards.

Rottweiler
45 days

Choosing and Raising Your Dog

Every person has a different idea of what makes an ideal canine companion: Some people prefer their dogs to be fawning and affectionate, and others like an independent, more reserved dog. Each breed has its own unique character, as does each dog. Choosing a dog is a complex and highly individual process, and you should take the same care as you would choosing a human companion.

Think carefully about the type of dog that you enjoy, and consider whether it is compatible with your lifestyle. You are looking for a good partner for yourself, but you must also be a good partner for your dog. If you'd like an active dog, you will need to have the space, time, and energy to be active with it. Many problems in raising and training result from an incompatibility between a dog's temperament and the environment of the household in which it is being asked to live.

When it comes to raising your dog, the terms "upbringing," "raising," and "training" are often used interchangeably, but there is a useful distinction to keep in mind. Formal training involves teaching a dog the skills to participate in competitions and dog shows; some people also call it training when they are teaching those ever-popular "dog tricks," like making a dog shake hands, walk on its hind legs, or raise one paw in greeting. However, neither of these things has anything to do with raising a dog.

Bringing up your dog means helping it develop the abilities it needs to live harmoniously in your household and in the world. It means socializing it so that it knows how to behave when it meets people other than those in your household. It means teaching it the proper etiquette for going out for a walk and how to respond to the basic behavioral commands, both for its own safety and the safety of others. It also means providing your dog with proper nutrition, a pleasant home, and a stimulating life.

There is no single, comprehensive method for raising a dog. Just as every set of parents has a different method for raising their children, so various styles of bringing up dogs can be effective. It all depends on the dog and the household. Be flexible, and take dog-training manuals with a grain of salt. Such iron-clad "rules" as "Morning and evening walks are a must," "The quantity of one meal should be about fist size," or "Don't allow dogs to defecate indoors" may not reflect the needs of you or your dog. Don't enforce arbitrary behaviors, and don't be afraid to try unique solutions.

Raising a dog properly is the owner's responsibility, and the owner must use his or her judgment to decide what's best. An owner cannot rely solely on a dog trainer, or slavishly follow a dog manual. In countless cases, dogs have learned to obey trainers, only to revert to their old, bad habits once they get home.

Dogs carefully observe their owners' behavior. Your dog will immediately pick up on your attitudes, and it will take advantage of you if you blame others when training doesn't go well, or if you enforce behaviors inconsistently or without conviction. A dog's training must be integrated into your everyday life, just as the dog itself needs to feel it is welcome and has a place in the home. As with children, puppies brought up by people who care for them wholeheartedly will grow to be happy, healthy adults, while those who are neglected or treated indifferently tend to be the ones with problems and issues.

The Basic Commands and a Few Common Issues

After consulting a dog manual, many people get overwhelmed. They often think, "I can't teach my dog all of these things. I don't think my dog could even do half of them." However, all dogs can learn basic social etiquette and walking manners, and beyond these you only need to teach your dog how to adapt to your household's specific rules.

One pitfall for new dog owners is the desire to teach tricks, so that the dog can show off and perform for others. This is usually done for the owner's benefit, not the dog's, and it is unnecessary training that will only confuse and stress your dog. Instead, the goal of training should be teaching your dog the skills it needs to have a joyous and relaxed life.

Collie
40 days

Alaskan malamute
50 days

In fact, the most basic goal of raising a dog is to prevent it from inflicting harm on others and itself, and nothing more. This is not difficult, but it cannot be done halfheartedly. As a dog owner, a life has been entrusted to you, and you must show it consistent care and attention. Raising a dog isn't just about adapting the animal to human ways, either. One often ends up rethinking one's own ways of living, with happy results.

The Five Basic Commands

Consider how your dog spends its days. In the morning, a person may take a shower, but a dog probably just stretches. Thereafter, a dog may eat and excrete, but while its owner is at work outside the home, a dog has nothing special to do. If someone else is home, it may follow or play with this person for a while, but most of the afternoon is spent resting. (Puppies may sleep up to 20 hours a day.)

When the owner finally comes home, he or she may play with the dog, exercise it a little, feed it, and take it out to excrete again before everyone goes to sleep. This routine is repeated daily—with occasional special trips to the beach or the woods—

and it amounts to a simple life. Dogs don't need to be taught how to do very much. Within their daily routine, all the necessary obedience training can occur. And that's how often training should happen, every day.

Just five commands—"Heel," "Sit," "Stay," "Down," and "Come"—are required for the minimal upbringing of a household dog. Heel is used to keep your dog from pulling on a leash or running ahead during a walk.

Sit, Stay, and Down are three different ways to get the dog to stop or be still. Sit might be used when there is a pause during a walk, such as while waiting for a traffic light to change, or when you want to curb the dog's instinct to chase something. Stay is used in a variety of situations, but especially when you must walk away from the dog and you don't want it to follow. It might also be used to calm a dog before giving it a treat or a meal. Down is often used in the home when you want the dog to lie down for an extended time while other activity is going on, such as during a meal or while watching television.

Come is the all-purpose command for getting your dog to come to you when you need it.

Enthusiasm, positive reinforcement, and consistency are the most important elements for teaching your dog to learn and obey these commands. Don't hesitate to exaggerate

your approval whenever your dog successful responds to one. If the dog learns that obeying commands leads to a happy outcome—such as your verbal approval, a friendly rub, or a treat—then it will eventually respond to your call automatically and without hesitation.

Nip Biting in the Bud

The first fundamental rule a dog must learn is not to bite.

When puppies bite playfully, say, "Ouch! No!" and look injured in an exaggerated way. Teach puppies it is absolutely unacceptable to bite a person.

Some puppies bite on table legs and electric cords, and this should also be stopped. Immediately substitute bones and toys, to make it clear exactly what the puppy is allowed to bite. Biting is a natural instinct, but you need to teach your dog what is acceptable to bite and what is not.

It is important to redirect biting early. Once a puppy reaches puberty, it will enter a rebellious stage, and uncontrolled biting can cause injury. Once a puppy is an adult, it is very hard to correct a biting habit.

Italian greyhound
50 days

Standard schnauzer
50 days

Old English
Sheepdog
30 days

The Streetwise Dog

Aside from disease, traffic accidents are the most frequent cause of death for dogs. Thus, teaching your dog not to suddenly dash into the street is another fundamental rule.

It is essential to teach your dog to obey your instruction of Stay. Even with a very obedient dog, you should never let it off its leash while walking along city or suburban streets. You can't always anticipate what will make a dog bolt, or stop it quickly enough when it does.

Some dogs are very sensitive to loud sounds, such as thunder and car engines, and they may panic and start barking or running when they hear them. Sometimes they even react to sounds human ears cannot detect. If your dog seems scared, rather than picking it up in your arms, tell it to sit. Soothe the dog by talking in a reassuring tone, and if it is big, put your arm around its neck to help calm it.

A panicked dog can become confused, and it may bite or become aggressive. Dogs in this state are uncontrollable. If you see signs that your dog is about to panic, move it away from the sound.

Housebreaking Your Dog

Just as children are taught to use the toilet, your dog should be taught to excrete in a specified place. This is the first challenge you will face when you own a dog. Note that it usually takes at least a hundred days before a dog is housebroken.

A puppy learns quite easily where to excrete if training is started around the time of weaning and you consistently take it to a set place. Unfortunately, breeders and pet shops commonly allow puppies to excrete freely.

Confining your puppy to a small space in your home helps it learn to restrict its excretions to a certain area outside. Puppies who are allowed to run loose in the home and are merely told where the toilet area is will not be able to comprehend. When your puppy uses the allocated area, praise it enthusiastically. If it makes a mistake, however, don't scold it; doing so will make it think the act of excreting is bad.

If your puppy sniffs and circles restlessly outside the designated area, take it to its area immediately. Praise its success, and excuse its failure if it cannot wait until it reaches the area. After your puppy learns to use only the appropriate area, gradually expand its range. However, if it consistently cannot reach its area in time, start over with a smaller or closer area.

Be patient, and don't give up until your puppy is thoroughly housebroken. Housebreaking failure is almost always the owner's fault. It is important not to give up too soon; be persistent and keep believing your dog will succeed.

Finally, don't believe you have to take your dog out to excrete. Why not provide a toilet space in the home? Just like people and cats, dogs can have a toilet area where they live, regardless of whether they are kept outdoors or indoors. Once your puppy learns to use its toilet area in the home, it is not necessary to take it outside in wet or cold weather or at night.

A Bark Is as Bad as a Bite

Dogs bark to communicate, but they should not be permitted to do so indiscriminately. Since dogs have many reasons for barking, some of which are justified, this problem should be dealt with according to each specific situation.

If you have an outdoor dog who persists in barking, do not bring it in the house. Doing so only teaches it that if it keeps barking, it will be brought indoors. Choose whether to keep your dog indoors or outdoors, and keep to your decision. If you decide to keep it outdoors, scold it sternly if it doesn't stop barking. Then, return indoors and watch what happens. As with housebreaking, this type of training is an endurance contest.

An indoor dog may keep barking when it doesn't get what it wants. Deal with this in the same way. Many people are afraid to scold their dogs, but it is essential to teach them clearly what is bad behavior. Don't abuse them, but don't hesitate to be firm.

Give Your Dog Its Space

Cover your dog's cage, basket, or space with a blanket, creating a dark, denlike environment—remember that dogs are descended from canids and once lived in burrows and caves—and put a bone or one of its favorite toys inside. Keep the entrance open so it can go in and out freely. This is its house.

If your dog's space is set up like this, it will like being there. If, however, the dog is forced to go there or is sent there when it is not wanted, it will not consider its space as a happy, comfortable place. Therefore, be sure to make the dog's space a place where your dog loves to stay and feels secure.

Many people teach their dog to go into its own area at the sound of a command, but this works and is acceptable only if the dog already feels comfortable there; each individual dog and the situation should be taken into consideration.

Furthermore, if you have company, put your dog in its space before your guests arrive. It is not pleasant for the dog if it senses that you and your company are having fun while it is being told to go to its space. It will feel left out and see the space as a place of banishment.

Puppy Puberty

Just like people, dogs go through puberty, which is a problematic stage. Small dogs enter puberty at 5 to 6 months, and it lasts until they are about 1 year old; for large dogs, puberty lasts from around 7 months to 1½ years. You will know when your dog enters puberty, as female puppies will begin menstruating, and male puppies will begin urinating with one leg lifted up.

During this period, all dogs become nervous and excitable, but this is also the time when they demonstrate their innate nature most clearly. Because of this, puberty is the most opportune time to establish a trusting relationship with your dog. Observe your dog carefully. Assess its nature and respond to it. If your adolescent dog is shy, help it develop a sense of security. If it is aggressive, deal with it sternly.

To some degree, all dogs are expected to become rebellious during this period, and they require solid teaching. If you neglect your dog or fail to deal with it properly while it's going through puberty, your relationship may be harmed in the long run.

All Dogs Need Training, Even Clever Ones

I often come across owners who proudly say, "Our dog is bright." But what are the signs of a dog's intelligence? Most owners call cheerful, friendly dogs that wag their tails for everyone "bright." (This type of dog is typical of the Toy and Sporting Groups.) However, these are simply sociable dogs. On the other hand, stubborn, self-assertive dogs that are not very friendly tend to be less favored. (These are typically found among Japanese and German breeds.) In between these two main character types exist a range of personalities, but one is not "better" or smarter than another. Choosing breeds is a matter of preference, and only with proper training does a dog learn how to express itself, and its intelligence, in the human world.

When I visit dogs at their home after one training session, some hide behind a door and spy on me. To me, these are clever dogs.

They are clearly thinking, "When she holds the leash, I have to obey her. I prefer my owner, because he lets me do whatever I like. I wish she would leave soon."

When I tell their owners their dogs are "clever," what I mean is that they can read situations and people,

American cocker spaniel 40 days

though I don't always know how owners interpret the word. These dogs often run the household, and they are wary when somebody more assertive steps in. What I would call clever dogs often need even more consistent training than others.

Human individuality begins when one learns to express oneself to the world and in social situations. Our parents and schools help us understand how to interact in the world, but individuality only develops fully when we become responsible for ourselves. Only when we have internalized society's rules can we give shape to our own choices and personality.

What about dogs? I believe a dog that has been taught the rules for living in human society and has no trouble living with people has individuality. It has the means for expressing its true nature. Dogs brought up properly more easily obey social rules, and they learn to express themselves within those rules. To bring a dog to this point, humans play the part of the dog's parents, teaching it everything it will need to know as it grows from a puppy into an adult dog.

Saluki 60 days

The Danger of Your Dog Becoming Your Master

In any pack of dogs, there is always one top dog. This phenomenon is an expression of their survival instinct. You may, in fact, think of it as natural wisdom coded in your dog's DNA.

Dogs today have little choice but to live in human society, but this wisdom still functions. Dogs will consider any collection of humans and other animals they live with as constituting the "pack." If a dog lives in a household with four humans and a cat, the pack consists of six members, including the dog, and each member has a rank. Canine society is hierarchical, and a dog will observe the group's dynamics to evaluate where it stands.

If a dog judges that it is at the top of this hierarchy, it will behave as the leader of the household pack. To the dog's understanding, all other members are lower in rank. When this becomes the case, training and upbringing become meaningless. The dog will become selfish and obey no one. A battle between the dog and its owners is inevitable.

How do you recognize when a dog has decided that its fellow household members are lower in rank? When you see a dog basically dragging its owner around while the person commands, "No! Heel!" When a dog does not listen, and the owner has to keep running after it.

Or, when a dog barks, growls, and becomes aggressive even to the extent of biting members of its own household. This dog thinks it is the top dog and believes others will obey if it displays aggression.

These dogs are unfortunate.

Hierarchies exist in human society, too, of course. However, a dog cannot truly become a top dog in human society. Thus, a dog that believes it is the top dog will only suffer, becoming unhappy, stressed out, and resorting to aggressive behavior.

Your dog cannot prepare meals for your household. It cannot go out, kill wild game, and bring it home. In domesticated environments, no outlet exists for a dog's survival instincts, so a dog that is top dog will only become irritable.

Owners make a mistake when they hold up their dogs above everything else. Your life must come first, and you must make clear to the dog that you are in charge. If your dog deliberately misbehaves or makes threats and you accommodate the

Face Value

Dogs are very expressive. When they think they have made a mistake, their faces say, "I goofed!" When they are happy, it is clear in their facial expression. Meanwhile, other expressions can imply potential problems with a dog's living environment. For example, stone-faced dogs are most likely neglected dogs. If you ignore a dog's wishes and needs, it will either become aggressive or give up. A dog that chooses to give up will gradually become emotionless. Similarly, a dog with sparkling eyes often has character problems. It may be aggressive or, to the contrary, shy.

behavior or heed the threats, the dog will immediately assume the mantle of top dog and continue being aggressive.

If your dog misbehaves or does something dangerous, reprimand it immediately and sternly. However, if you come home and find that your dog has broken something in your absence, scolding won't do any good because the dog will already have forgotten the incident.

When your dog growls at you, respond resolutely; it is the same as your child talking back to you. Don't mollify or coddle the dog by asking, "Are you in a bad mood? What can I do for you?" Deal properly with a growling dog before it becomes a biting dog. When dogs bite, I blame the owner, not the dog. It is ultimately the owner's responsibility to teach a dog how to control its behavior.

Remember, a dog will be more sociable when it accepts its standing as one of the house's members rather than its leader. And it will ultimately be much happier.

Airedale Terrier
78 days

Dogo Argentino

Learning with Dogs

Generally, when I train dogs, I expect their owners to participate. I once thought it was easier to train dogs without their owners present, but I realize now I was mistaken. I had overlooked the fact that the lives of dogs are spent with their owners and within the field of their owners' activities. Since I realized this, I have been training dogs in their home environments. The members of the household see what I do, and I ask them to do the same. By observing and imitating me, they are better able to comprehend my motives and methods.

It is all too common for people to ask a dog trainer to train their dog without making adjustments in their lives: If this happens, as soon as your dog returns to your home, it will be back to square one. If you, as your dog's owner, do not adapt to its presence, it will not be able to adapt either. In these cases, if a trainer revisits the home of a dog he or she has trained, the dog will behave properly again because the trainer has already established the proper relationship. Dogs will change their behavior according to who handles them.

To a dog, a trainer is a figure it cannot control, thus he or she is given respect. At the same time, the dog comes to love its trainer because it understands that everything the trainer does is in its best interests.

Its trainer is teaching it how to live in human society, teaching clear distinctions between good and bad by praising it when it does something good and scolding it when it does something bad. Once the dog understands that its trainer is motivated by love and concern, it will listen and obey.

This is true of anyone. We feel good when we are with someone who understands us, and we enjoy communicating with that person. When a dog feels that its trainer is attuned to it, it responds willingly, eager to communicate and learn.

You don't have to be a professional trainer to do this. Give a dog your undivided attention, and the dog will listen to you. Teach a dog with love, care, and enthusiasm, and the dog will learn. Be sensitive to your dog's emotional needs, and your dog will be happy and easy to handle. Unfortunately, some owners can be insensitive to or ignorant of their dog's needs, and they only ever ask, "Does it want to play?" "Is it hungry?"

The needs of dogs are far more complex. Their lives might seem to consist solely of eating, playing, and sleeping, but they need emotional care as well. Your dog wants to communicate with you, and by observing your dog's expressions and behavior every day, you will become sensitive to these efforts. And by consistently conveying your wishes through the tone of your voice, your dog will come to understand you, too.

Much training consists of giving some kind of reward for good behavior—like a food treat or toy—and reprimanding or withholding for bad behavior. This "carrot and stick" approach is useful, and it works. Your dog will certainly pay attention if you dangle a carrot in front of it. However, at the same time you should establish heart-to-heart communication with your dog. If you can do this, the carrot will become unnecessary, and your dog will respond to you because it knows that it is understood and loved, and it will be eager to return both those things to you.

Afghan Hound
40 days

How To Raise Healthy Dogs

By Masahiko Noya, Director of Noya Animal Hospital

What Constitutes a Dog's Health?

It is difficult to discern whether a dog is healthy or ill. With a person, it is relatively easy to see if he or she lacks an appetite, is walking more slowly, is short of breath, or seems to be irritable or to have a fever, but a dog does not always show obvious signs of sickness.

You must watch your dog closely, and be very attuned to its appearance and behavior, in order to tell if something is wrong. Dogs need the same level of monitoring that human babies do, since neither can communicate very well about their own condition.

Surprisingly, many owners don't seem to observe their dogs closely enough. Usually, by the time changes in a dog's health have become obvious, the sickness has reached an advanced stage. It is crucial that an owner pick up even subtle shifts in his or her dog's health because, by the time the changes are noticeable, it may be too late. Internal health problems are especially difficult to recognize.

Because of this, regular visits with a veterinarian are very important. Most dogs should go at least once a year, and older dogs twice a year. Of course, don't be oversensitive about your dog's health, but be attentive, and don't hesitate to check with your vet if you suspect something is wrong.

Finally, just as each dog has its own personality, each breed has its own health characteristics and problems. These are the various diseases, afflictions, and defects that are the sometimes negative consequences of selective breeding. You will be at an advantage if you know beforehand which, if any, occur frequently among the breed of dog you would like as a pet. (See the list of these conditions by breed on page 221.)

Chihuahuas
56 days

Basic Principles of Keeping Dogs Healthy

Just as they are for people, the main culprits in health problems for dogs are poor diet, insufficient physical activity, and stress. In the simplest terms, keeping your dog healthy means providing it with good nutrition, sufficient activity, and a safe and loving home.

While people can evaluate the taste and quality of their drinking water and decide whether they'll drink from the tap, use a filter, or buy bottled water, dogs must drink what we give them or suffer from thirst. As such, dog owners should exercise the same judgment in the case of their dog's drinking water as they use for their own.

Similarly, dogs must eat what we give them, and not all dog foods are alike. It is important to research which ones provide the most nutritional value and the least unnecessary or unhealthy ingredients—or, better, no unhealthy ingredients at all.

As for how much your dog should eat at each meal, the rule of thumb is to give it an amount of food equal to the size of a fist. However, appetites vary based on a dog's size, its health, and the amount of exercise it gets. To decide the appropriate amount of food, you will need to observe your dog and use your judgment. Experiment with different kinds and combinations of food until your dog consistently eats well, but vary the portions according to its needs.

The amount of exercise a dog needs also varies, both by breed and the individual. The physical capabilities of sled dogs in Alaska and the North Arctic—who can run tens of miles a day in severe winter conditions—seem inconceivable, but many breeds perform similarly exceptional feats of strength and endurance. Owners often don't know the capabilities of their dogs, and without thinking they simply make them conform to human standards, in a sense confining them. For the sake of your dog's health, it should be allowed to exercise according to its needs, not yours.

The standard guide for how much daily exercise a dog needs is to allow it to walk about one-fourth of a mile for every pound it weighs. This is a rough estimate, but if you cannot walk your dog, especially a large one, at least this much, you should not own it.

However, calculating mileage is less important than knowing your dog's breed and using common sense: Hound dogs bred to run all day, for example, should not be kept on a rope in a small yard. Before you decide on a puppy, make sure your lifestyle and environment are compatible with what the dog's needs will be as an adult.

Overall, you can get a basic idea of a dog's fitness by feeling its body. You should barely be able to feel its ribs and hipbones. If those parts seem to be sticking out, your dog is too skinny. If you cannot feel them, your dog is obese. Ideally, a dog should be of moderate build, neither too thin nor too fat.

English pointer
29 days

Some Common Ailments

Not every ailment is an emergency. Like people, dogs will get sick for a day or two and recover, and there is sometimes little we can do but comfort them until they feel better. At some point in time, your dog is likely to suffer from fever, diarrhea, constipation, or vomiting. If one of these happens, monitor the condition closely; the rule of thumb is that if a condition persists for more than two days, call a veterinarian.

However, if several symptoms occur together (particularly vomiting and diarrhea), or if you have some other reason for thinking your dog might be suffering a serious illness, don't wait two days to seek help. When in doubt, always call your vet immediately.

It can be hard to determine if a dog has a fever, but if yours seems to have one, do not randomly administer medication. If the fever seems extremely high, you could try to bring it down by placing a bag of ice or some other cooling agent on your dog's stomach. Take your dog to a veterinarian if the fever does not subside in a day.

If your dog has diarrhea, check to make sure the stool is not bloody or watery. If it is, call a vet immediately. Otherwise, put your dog on a fast. Dogs do not digest grains efficiently, and oily meals create film on the intestinal lining that hinders the intestines from absorbing water. Monitor your dog's health for the next 12 to 24 hours. If the diarrhea subsides, feed your dog something other than grains, oily food, or milk. If it persists, take your dog to the vet.

In general, short-term constipation should not concern you, but check with a vet if it lasts more than a week. However, if your dog cannot defecate even though it strains to the point of yelping from pain, a hernia or a serious disease may be responsible; if this seems to be the case, see your veterinarian.

If your dog vomits but appears well and eats again at the next mealtime, it is likely there is no problem. However, if it vomits repeatedly in one day, or several times over the course of a week, something is probably wrong, and you should see a vet.

If your dog vomits when its stomach is empty, this can be a sign of gastric hyperacidity, which is usually solved by giving your dog smaller, more frequent portions of food so there is always food in its stomach. Check with your vet to establish a feeding routine that will ensure that your dog's calorie intake remains sufficient.

The Hair of the Dog

Many dog owners think that trimming the coat of a long-haired dog helps it bear warm weather, but this is a dangerous misconception. Each breed has developed the hair quality and density best fit for the environment and climate in which it was bred, and the coat that is characteristic of each breed evolves over many generations before it reaches its present state.

The basic role of hair is to regulate body temperature. In the summer, long hair protects a dog's skin from direct sunlight and helps lower the skin temperature. In winter, it sustains body heat. These functions would be lost if a long-haired dog were trimmed.

Another misconception is the belief that it's better to shampoo your dog in the sunlight so its coat will dry more quickly. If a dog is left to dry in the sun, some water and shampoo may remain under the coat, which will irritate the skin later and cause itching. Your dog may lick the skin to relieve the itching, which may result in a hot spot or acute moist dermatitis. In particular, dogs belonging to breeds with water-resistant hair, such as golden retrievers, should be shampooed in cool, airy shade. Then, dry the coat and skin thoroughly with a towel. Also, use water warmed to about 88 to 91 degrees Fahrenheit.

Chow chow
39 dayshh

Diseases by Breed

Breed	Diseases, Afflictions, and Defects
Herding Group	
Australian kelpie	Involutional microphthalmia
Australian shepherd	Umbilical hernia; microphthalmia; deafness
Bearded collie	Persistence of pupillary membrane; epilepsy
Belgian sheepdog	Epilepsy; lymphedema
Border collie	Primary ciliary dysfunction (prone to pneumonia)
Bouvier des Flandres	Laryngeal paralysis
Cardigan Welsh corgi	Generalized progressive retinal degeneration; retina dysplasia
Collie	Collie eye; solar dermatitis
German shepherd	Harelip; hemophilia A
Old English sheepdog	Detachment of retina; hypoplasia of hip joint (severe case)
Pembroke Welsh corgi	Dermatomyositis; retina dysplasia
Shetland sheepdog	Hemophilia A; thyroid insufficiency
Sporting Group	
American cocker spaniel	Phosphofructokinase deficiency (anoxia); kneecap dislocation; seborrhea
Brittany spaniel	Complement deficiency (deficiency of blood protein)
Clumber spaniel	Inertia uteri; undershot; loss of permanent teeth
English cocker spaniel	Cryptorchid; swimmer puppy
English pointer	Panosteitis (otitis); umbilical hernia
English setter	Inertia uteri; hemophilia A
English springer spaniel	Cutaneous asthenia
Flat-coated retriever	None
Golden retriever	Hypoplasia of hip joint; bilateral cataract; hemophilia A
Irish setter	Quadriplegia accompanied by amblyopia
Labrador retriever	Seborrhea; thyroid insufficiency; cystinuria (prone to developing stones); hemophilia A
Nova Scotia duck tolling retriever	None
Weimaraner	Hemophilia A; undershot; dilatation of stomach
Hound Group	
Afghan hound	Afghan myelomalacia
Basenji	Fanconi syndrome; inguinal hernia; umbilical hernia
Basset hound	Platelet disorder; achondroplasia of limbs
Beagle	Thyroid insufficiency; cutaneous asthenia; alopecia universalis; intervertebral disk hernia
Borzoi	Lymphedema; progressive retinal degeneration
Dachshund	Renal disease; intervertebral disk hernia; thyroid insufficiency; eye disease
Irish wolfhound	Synovial cyst of the elbows; sinus syndrome
Petit basset griffon Vendéen	Hypothyroidism; allergies; epilepsy
Saluki	Detachment of retina; barbituric drug sensitivity
Whippet	None
Terrier Group	
Airedale terrier	Cerebellar hypoplasia; umbilical hernia
Bedlington terrier	Osteogenesis imperfecta
Border terrier	None
Bull terrier	Recessive umbilical hernia; inguinal hernia
Cairn terrier	Inguinal hernia (high risk); pseudohemophilia
Jack Russell terrier	None
Kerry Blue terrier	Cerebellar nutrition disorder
Lakeland terrier	Dislocation of the lens; undershot; cryptorchid
Miniature schnauzer	Von Willebrand's disease; Legg-Calve-Perthes' disease; bladder stone; thyroid insufficiency
Norfolk terrier	None
Scottish terrier	Volvulus of the stomach
Sealyham terrier	Ectopia lentis
Soft-coated wheaten terrier	Postretinal degeneration; dermatitis
Welsh terrier	None
West Highland white terrier	Atopic dermatitis; cardiac disease; hypoplasia of hip joint
Wire fox terrier	Ataxia; severe myasthenia

Breed	Diseases, Afflictions, and Defects
Toy Group	
Brussels griffon	Dislocation of the shoulder; trichiasis
Cavalier King Charles spaniel	Cardiac disease; diabetes mellitus; falling soft palate; kneecap dislocation
Chihuahua	Tracheal collapse; hemophilia A; hydrocephalia
Chinese crested	None
Italian greyhound	Epilepsy; monorchidism
Japanese chin	Harelip syndrome; cleft palate syndrome; esophageal hiatus hernia; monorchidism
Maltese	Hydrocephalia; hypoglycemia; monorchidism; cardiac disease; tracheal collapse
Manchester terrier	Diabetes; Legg-Calve-Perthes' disease
Miniature pinscher	Dislocation of the shoulder; Legg-Calve-Perthes' disease
Papillon	Anasarca; kneecap dislocation
Pekingese	Intervertebral disk disorder; inguinal hernia; umbilical hernia
Pomeranian	Tracheal collapse; cryptorchid; hair loss; kneecap dislocation; cardiac disease; cryptotestis
Pug	Delayed sunstroke; eye disease
Shih tzu	Cortex renis imperfecta; harelip
Yorkshire terrier	Dry eye syndrome; tracheal collapse; kneecap dislocation; Legg-Calve-Perthes' disease
Working Group	
Akita	Umbilical hernia; generalized progressive retinal degeneration; skin disease
Alaskan malamute	Recessive day blindness; hemophilia A
Bernese mountain dog	Low myelination/myelination failure
Boxer	Deafness; cutaneous asthenia
Bullmastiff	Cleft palate syndrome; abnormal dentation; vagina hyperplasia
Doberman pinscher	Cortex renis imperfecta
Dogo Argentino	None
Giant schnauzer	Hypoplasia of hip joint (frequent)
Great Dane	Cystinuria (prone to developing stones); necrotic myelitis
Great Pyrenees	Anophthalmia; fragility of bone syndrome
Leonberger	None
Newfoundland	Myocardiosis; strain fracture
Rottweiler	Diabetes; hypoplasia of hip joint
Saint Bernard	Stockyard paralysis; hemophilia A; hemophilia B
Samoyed	Hemophilia A; diabetes
Siberian husky	Pseudohemophilia; corneal dysplasia
Standard schnauzer	Hemophilia A; cataract; conjunctivitis
Non-Sporting Group	
Bichon frise	Epilepsy; dislocation of kneecap interior surface
Boston terrier	Cerebellar hypoplasia; water diabetes; hydrocephalia
Bulldog	Cystinuria; factor VII deficiency
Chow chow	Cleft-soft-palate syndrome; cleft-palate syndrome; hypoplasia of hip joint
Dalmatian	Uric acid stone; atopic dermatitis; nacilluria
French bulldog	Partial loss of vertebra; hemophilia A; hemophilia B
Lhasa apso	Agyria; cortex renis imperfecta; inguinal hernia
Poodle (standard)	Microphthalmia; atypical pannus; hemophilia A; pseudohemophilia
Poodle (toy and miniature)	Cushing's syndrome; hypersensitive dermatitis; achondroplasia; hemophilia A
Schipperke ease	Narrow palpebral fissure; Legg-Calve-Perthes' disease
Shar-pei	Constriction of external nostrils; selaphobia; hypoplasia of hip joint
Shiba inu	Pseudohyperkalemia; atopic dermatitis; kneecap dislocation
Tibetan spaniel	None

Glossary

■ Coat Color

Albino . . . . A dog that lacks pigment in skin and hair.

Apricot . . . . A reddish yellow coat color.

ASCOB . . . . An abbreviation of "Any solid color other than black" for coat color; used for the American cocker spaniel.

Beaver . . . . A beaverlike brown coat color.

Belton . . . . A white coat color with small frecklelike spots.

Biscuit . . . . A light fawn or light golden coat color that is close to cream.

Black and tan . . . . A black base coat color with tan spots above the eyes, on both sides of the muzzle, on the throat, on the lower parts of the legs, and around the anus.

Blaze . . . . A long, white stripe that runs from the nose to the forehead.

Blenheim . . . . A red and white coat color; that of the cavalier King Charles spaniel.

Blue . . . . A bluish gray coat color.

Blue merle . . . . . . A marbling of black, blue, and gray in the coat.

Brindle . . . . A coat with a base color in which hair of other colors is mixed.

Brown . . . . A coat color ranging from brown to liver.

Chestnut . . . . Chestnut brown coat color.

Chocolate . . . . . . Dark reddish brown or dark brown coat color.

Clouds . . . . Light-colored hair with black tips; that of the German shepherd.

Coat . . . . The hair that covers a dog.

Collar . . . . White hair around the neck.

Cream . . . . Milk white coat color.

Culottes . . . . Long, thick hair behind the thighs.

Dapple . . . . A coat with patterns in different colors.

Double coat . . . . . A coat that has both a topcoat and an undercoat.

Fawn . . . . A golden brown coat color, ranging from dark fawn mixed with black hair to yellowish fawn.

Feathering . . . . . . Long hair on the ears, neck, legs, and tail.

Gold . . . . Golden coat color; also called lion color.

Gray . . . . Ash coat color.

Grizzle . . . . Bluish gray coat color.

Harlequin . . . . Irregular black patches on a white-colored base coat; common with the Great Dane.

Honey . . . . A coat color resembling the color of honey.

Hound color . . . . . A coat color with black and brown patches on a white base color.

Isabella . . . . Light chestnut.

Landseer . . . . Black markings on a white base coat; the coat color of the Newfoundland. (Some kennel clubs recognize the Landseer as a separate breed.)

Lemon . . . . A yellow coat color.

Lion gold . . . . Reddish gold coat color that looks like lion hair.

Liver . . . . Dark reddish brown coat color, resembling the color of liver.

Mahogany . . . . . . Reddish chestnut coat color close to red brown.

Orange . . . . Mars yellow coat color, including light tan.

Parti-color . . . . . . A white coat with obvious one-color or two-color patches.

Pencil mark . . . . . Black lines that run on the digits of the Manchester terrier.

Plucking . . . . A trimming method used to pull hard hair out in the topcoat with a tool called a stripper.

Prince Charles . . . A tricolor coat color; that of the cavalier King Charles spaniel.

Reddish brown . . . Brown coat color with a red hue.

Red . . . . A reddish brown coat color, ranging from light red to yellowish red.

Roan . . . . A coat that has white hair mixed in with the base color.

Rough coat . . . . . . A medium-long coat.

Ruby . . . . A dark chestnut red; that of the cavalier King Charles spaniel.

Rust tan . . . . Brown coat color with a hue of rust.

Sable . . . . Yellowish brown coat color, or a coat in which black-tipped hair is mixed.

Salt-and-Pepper . . A coat color that looks like a mixture of salt and pepper. It ranges from bluish salt-and-pepper to light silver gray.

Sand . . . . A sandlike coat color; also called sand color, or sandy.

Sashi-ge . . . . Hair of a different color that is mixed in the topcoat.

Shade . . . . Whitish hair colored from its tip to halfway down.

Silver . . . . A grayish silver coat color.

Silver gray . . . . . . Gray coat color with a light silver hue.

Single coat . . . . . . A coat that does not have both a topcoat and an undercoat.

Smooth . . . . Short and straight coat hair.

Spot marking . . . . Black or liver patches on a white base coat, covering the entire body.

Steel blue . . . . A bluish copper coat color.

Stripping . . . . Plucking of unwanted or unnecessarily long hair from the topcoat.

Tan brown . . . . . . A coat color with two variations; light brown is called light tan, and dark brown is called rich tan.

Thumb marks . . . . Black spots on the forepaws.

Ticking . . . . A white coat with small patches in black or other colors.

Tiger color . . . . . . A fawn or gold coat with tigerlike stripes; also called tiger brindle or tiger hair.

Topcoat . . . . A top layer of hair; coarse and longer than the undercoat.

Tricolor . . . . A coat color that is black, tan, and white.

Undercoat . . . . . . A lower layer of hair; softer and shorter than the topcoat.

Wheaten . . . . A coat color resembling ripe wheat.

Whiskers . . . . Long hair on both sides of the muzzle and under the jaws.

Wire coat . . . . A coat of wiry hair with a hard topcoat.

Wolf . . . . Liver gray or yellow brown, with black cloud markings; also called wolf gray.

Yellow . . . . A wide range of coat colors from fox color to light yellow.

■ Mouth, Eyes, Ears, and Tail

Almond eye . . . . . Almond-shaped eyes.

Bat ear . . . . Round-tipped prick ears.

Circular eye . . . . . Round eyes.

Crank tail . . . . A cranklike short tail carried down with its tip slightly twisted upward.

Cropping . . . . Cutting off a portion of a puppy's ears to make them prick up.

Curled tail . . . . . . A tail curled and carried over the back.

Docking . . . . Cutting off a puppy's tail shot.

Hook tail . . . . A hanging tail with a curled-up tip.

Kink tail . . . . A short tail tightly twisted from the tail joint.

Muzzle . . . . The part of a dog's face that includes the nose and the mouth.

Oval eye . . . . Egg-shaped eyes.

Screw tail . . . . A very short tail that looks like a corkscrew.

Sickle tail . . . . A tail carried over the back without curling.

Stern tail . . . . A tail with relatively short hair, such as those typical of the Hound Group and the Terrier Group.

Stop . . . . The stepped part between the muzzle and the forehead.

Walleye . . . . Pale bluish eye color.

Index

Age Comparison of Humans and Dogs

Dog Years	Human Years
1 month	1 year
2 months	3 years
4 months	7 years
1 year	18 years
5 years	35 years
11 years	60 years
16 years	80 years

These proportions are rough estimates; also, the ratio varies according to breed size.

About the Authors

Hiroyuki Ueki

Ueki, born in Hyogo Prefecture, Japan, in 1955, became a freelance advertising photographer after working for a commercial photography studio for 9 years. A member of the Japan Professional Photographers Society, he is actively involved in photographing dogs and cats.

Toyofumi Fukuda

Fukuda, a freelance photographer born in Saga Prefecture, Japan, in 1955, photographs creatures such as mudskippers (fish that are able to propel themselves over mud and sand) along the sea of Ariake, near Kyushu, Japan. He also enjoys photographing dogs and cats.

In 1996, Ueki and Fukuda formed the company Office UFP, conducting joint photo shoots and publishing many books, including *Feelings of a Puppy and Feelings of Its Mother, Yama-Kei Pocket Guidebook: Cats & Dogs, Dog's Complaint, Cat's Excuse, Running Dogs: Dogs in the Winds,* and *Hound Dogs*.

Hiromi Nakano

Nakano, an author and editor of mostly children's natural-science books, coauthored *Number Two* and translated *The Dorling-Kindersley Guide to the Human Body*.

Tadaaki Imaizumi

Imaizumi, born in Tokyo in 1944, studied taxonomy and the ecology of mammals in general and participated in an ecological survey of the Iriomote wild cat and the Japanese river otter; his research also covers the dog and cat behavior. A former researcher with the Fuji Animal Park Association and animal commentator for the Ueno Zoo, he wrote *Iriomote Wild Cat on the Rarely Visited Islands of the Southern Sea, The Earth and Its Extinct Animals, Animals That Failed to Evolve, Encyclopedic Accounts of Wild Dogs,* and many other books.

Book Design and Layout by Akihiko Yokoyama (WSB)